OCD to Me

An Anthology of Anxieties

Ryan Bernstein

Published by Waldorf Publishing
2140 Hall Johnson Road
#102-345
Grapevine, Texas 76051
www.WaldorfPublishing.com

OCD to Me
An Anthology of Anxieties

ISBN: 978-1-64255-038-2
Library of Congress Control Number: 2018904623

Dedication

This book is dedicated to anyone who battles with OCD, as well as the friends and loved ones who support them.

All proceeds from book sales will be donated to the International OCD Foundation.

Table of Contents

Foreword: My Postpartum OCD

Jenny C. Yip, Psy.D., ABPP

Shared stories of our struggles can be both enlightening and empowering, while giving hope to those who may also be suffering. Stories can raise awareness, defuse ignorance, motivate others to take action, and even bring people and communities together to effect change. It gives us, the story holders, the opportunity to recognize and embrace our own strengths through our trials and tribulations. When we look back, take a deep breath, and exhale a long sigh of relief, we realize with amazement of where we've been and how far we've come.

My own trials and tribulations with OCD have expanded close to 40 years. Though I have had many battles with OCD, some where I won and others where my OCD Monster got the better of me, they all seem far and distant. OCD is a prankster. It has a way of tricking you into dismissing it and the arduous exposure work needed, because you believe you have defeated it for good. When you are disarmed and least expect it, OCD comes knocking with a newer, oftentimes more convoluted challenge. And once again, you must rediscover your tools and strength to go back into the battleground with this nuisance.

After all of the battles I've encountered with my OCD Monster, where do I begin my story? I could talk about my childhood washing and showering days, where my parents later joked about wishing they had given me the water bill as a deterrent. Or I could describe the time I was three hours late to my own 16th birthday party from being stuck with symmetry compulsions. Truthfully, I could begin anywhere; however, I believe the most impactful story I can share may come from a lesser known or talked about subtype: Postpartum OCD.

My boys recently turned one. As I reminisce over the past year, I'm reminded of the challenges of the initial days, weeks, even months after my loves were born. Although the experience of having newborn twins and motherhood in general was insane, it was still manageable. Juggling multiple tasks under very little sleep was not new to me. What wasn't manageable was the unexpected return of my OCD.

Having battled obsessive-compulsive disorder since the age of four, finally triumphing over it in my 20s, and later becoming a specialist in treating the most severe cases of OCD, I was shocked at the devastating effect OCD had on me once again. Not only was I overly arrogant that I had defeated OCD for good, the thought of experiencing OCD postpartum never even crossed my mind. Surely, I have treated many women suffering from postpartum OCD. And like most people who have overcome OCD, I've had minor intrusive thoughts here and there that were now easily ignored. However, being deeply trapped in intrusive thoughts of potential harm to my loved ones, along with silly magical compulsions to ensure their safety was a thing of the past, so I thought. I was wrong.

Within the first week after my boys were born, OCD reared its ugly head once again. This time, it was clever as ever disguising itself in nebulous form. The OCD Monster is a shape-shifter. A trickster. I knew this. Despite presenting itself again in the OCD category of potential harm to others, it *felt* different this time. The intrusive thoughts were more elusive, creative and obscure. Even

I, the OCD specialist, could not see it for what it was. My OCD had become trickier and more cunning than I ever remembered.

My fear was that I would love one twin more than the other, and in some weird OCD way, would cause harm to their emotional development. To neutralize this intrusive obsession, I drove myself crazy ensuring that everything I did for one of the boys was EXACTLY the same as the other. From something as mundane as how each bottle gets scrubbed to the more complicated measurement of skin-to-skin contact, OCD dug its claws into just about every facet of motherhood. Breastfeeding became the most taxing task. How does one even quantify how much milk exactly each infant got? Was there a specific mathematical formula? Length of time x Rate of sucking x Milk production x Time of day = You get the idea of the insanity of OCD.

Making matters even more exhausting, I spent each night checking my memory bank for the number of times I thought of each twin, comparing the content and emotional context of each thought. All of this was in vain, just to say I loved them equally. I drove myself insane. Or put more correctly, OCD drove me insane. Did I have the common postpartum OCD symptoms of excessive handwashing, sanitizing baby bottles, and checking for the babies' safety? Yes, I had those too. The skin on my hands was once again chapped, cracked, and raw. Clean bottles couldn't touch anything unsanitized. And I had to touch my babies' chests to make sure I felt them rise and fall. Seeing that they were breathing while asleep wasn't enough. This was how I spent the first few months of motherhood – bliss turned into torment.

Unfortunately, there is little information on postpartum OCD or its symptoms, especially within the medical community where a postnatal woman would be screened. Women are regularly screened for and educated about postpartum depression at prenatal and postnatal visits. However, research indicates that as many as 10-50% of new mothers actually suffer from postpartum OCD, which is often misdiagnosed as postpartum depression.

Symptoms tend to be intense, appear out of the blue, and are similar to those in others suffering from OCD. Sadly, many mothers often suffer alone for fear of disclosing the offensive nature of their symptoms and receiving negative judgment from others. Some women have even been involuntarily hospitalized by doctors with a lack of awareness of postpartum OCD. Fortunately, as with other types of OCD, postpartum OCD is very treatable with Exposure and Response Prevention Therapy (ERP).

My own ERP was just as torturous as the ones I prescribe to my patients. I had to visualize and imagine the unbearable possibility of harm befalling my sweet, innocent babies. I had to live with the uncertainty of not knowing what might happen to them one day. I had to accept the reality that they could die before I do. These thoughts would be hard to swallow for any parent. For those of us with OCD, we must repeat these exposures until the painful thoughts lose their power. That is the only way to be free from the chains of OCD, so that motherhood *can* be bliss without OCD's torment.

Although exposing yourself to your worst fears is a daunting task, living with the agonizing thoughts of OCD is much, much worse. At least exposures are short-term with long-term relief. Having to live with OCD without proper treatment is life-long. One that I would never be willing to tolerate. I chose to be free from OCD, so that I could bond authentically with my boys without OCD's interference. As I now reflect back on those early days suffering from postpartum OCD, the arduous exposures have been worth every tear and heartbreak.

With this recent battle, I am once again reminded of the value of the tools I have for overcoming any new challenge my OCD Monster may bring. I am also reminded of my own strength and perseverance for defeating this nuisance. In reality, doing exposures to confront OCD gives me the power and removes it from the prankster. Sometimes I win. Sometimes I don't. Like most things in life, as long as I am determined and have the skillset, I know I will conquer whatever obstacle that stands in front of me. And OCD is no exception.

Chapter One: Ryan's Story

I don't recall a time during my childhood or teenage years that I ever felt relaxed. I don't mean the sitting in the lounge chair on a sandy beach in the sunshine kind of relaxed. I mean mentally relaxed. My mind has always been in motion. That fight or flight feeling of anxiety, of unsettled nerves, of edgy uncomfortableness is a constant companion. This "mental moodiness" as it was often described because of its variability was baffling to my family, to my doctors, to my teachers, and most of all, to me. No one could figure out why I was so miserable. To make matters more difficult, as I grew up my "mental moodiness" showed itself in many different ways.

I come from an in-tact close-knit family. I have an older brother. I live next door to my grandparents. My uncle and aunt and cousins live down the street. On the surface everything should have been perfect. I was reading at the age of three. By five I was playing complicated piano sonatas. I loved learning new things, but had trouble going to pre-school. I didn't like leaving my familiar surroundings. It was really difficult to go, and I remember being frequently pulled off of my mom crying as the door closed behind me. The doctors chalked it up to age-appropriate separation anxiety. The school administrators chalked it up to being really smart. They figured I was bored so that was why I didn't want to go to school. They thought if I was more engaged in my learning I wouldn't miss my mom, so they decided to bump me up a grade. They moved me mid-year into the kindergarten class. Things improved a bit. School was a bit more fun but not very challenging. I still didn't like the unfamiliar and I still had trouble leaving my mom.

By grade school things got worse. I didn't like bright lights. I hated loud noises. I never looked people in the eye. I had trouble making friends and got picked on a lot. The doctors said I was just shy. They asked my mom if she was shy. She was. They asked my dad if he was shy. He was. They said it was a family trait, and that parents who are nervous and shy often have kids who are nervous and shy. The school administrators just thought I was still bored, which to be fair, I was, and so they decided to give me a lot of advanced schoolwork to do. But they still didn't know what was going on. It was so much more than the schoolwork. In fact, there were too many things that made me feel uncomfortable. I didn't like to be in close proximity to other people. I didn't like sharing pencils and rulers and other school supplies. I wanted to sit in the same spot every day and I wanted my space clean. I didn't like changing from one activity to another. Once I was settled I wanted to stay not move from room to room or building to building for my different classes. But the worst part of my day was lunch period. It was the worst part of the day because it combined all of the things that made me feel anxious into one event. I didn't like all of the chaos and the noise and then trying to find a place to sit with all of the different grades bumping and jostling and filling the space. It was awful.

And then things got even worse. The summer of third grade I couldn't eat. I don't know why, but I just couldn't. My mom tried everything from special cereals, to hot dogs, to French fries, to soup, to pudding. I even could eat with the TV on, but nothing worked. I lost a lot of weight. The doctors said it was just a phase. Kids are picky eaters. Had I always been a picky eater? Yes. Was

I someone who stayed with the familiar or was I an adventurous eater? I was definitely the former. Well, it will pass. Don't worry, they reassured my mom.

It didn't. By fourth grade I spent one hundred and twenty arduous days eating only dried rice cereal for lunch. In sixth grade, I wouldn't even eat at school. The teachers would ask me if I ate, and I would have to make up an excuse because I felt embarrassed. At home I felt angry and lonely. No one understood what I was feeling. To be honest, even I didn't really know why I was so upset. The doctors said it was the moodiness of puberty. But it felt like so much more than that. I didn't want to go anywhere. I didn't want to talk to anyone. I felt agitated all the time. I worried a lot about everything from using too much paper to what was going on in the world to why it was raining so much to where my brother was.

By seventh grade, I was afraid to go to school and needed my mom to stand outside the classroom. I would cry and visibly shake at the thought of going to school. My school was a nice, small, supportive place and I felt panic every minute when I was there. Why? I had no idea. The doctors ran tests. I was in the 99% of every test they ran. Words like gifted, intellectual, genius, perfectionist, challenging, floated around. But no one seemed to be able to help me, although they tried to lend support by rationalizing my thoughts. "Everyone feels anxious at times," they would say. "It's normal to feel frustrated at times. It's most likely stress. It's just a teenage stage," they would say. "Will it be over soon?" I would say.

By eighth grade, just thinking about being at school made me so nervous that when I went, I always wore my hood up. I started wearing mittens to school year-round. I always wore shorts and a short-sleeved shirt regardless of the weather. I still couldn't eat at school. I still didn't like to share a desk or a pencil. I still needed my area clean. I still didn't like noise, being around lots of people, or a change in my routine. I still felt upset, uncomfortable, and anxious. I had trouble sleeping because my brain would never shut off. The doctors thought I had non-specified anxiety and suggested I see a child behavior therapist on a regular basis. I couldn't attend without my mom going in with me. I was too nervous. My mom would talk, and I would sit with my hood pulled up around my head saying nothing. I had nothing to say. The therapist liked to talk about the past. I was suffering in the present. We didn't get very far.

Instead my mom tried a long and creative laundry list of activities and therapies to help me feel safe. The house always smelled of lavender, a calming scent. We increased my variety of physical activities: swimming (the thought was that floating would be freeing), rock climbing (the thought was that conquering tall walls and boulders would make me feel confident), taekwondo (the thought was that if I learned to protect myself I'd feel secure). I took art classes with the hope that I could visually depict my fears through clay, colored paints, or charcoal pencils. I also learned new musical instruments. Music is good for the brain, so I challenged myself with the violin, the recorder, the clarinet, and the guitar. Music also wound its way through my days. Soothing melodies and happy tunes were supposed to keep me feeling good and were played in the car as well as in my room. There was also meditation and jungle gym yoga (that was really different!) to engage my mind and keep it from traveling down darker paths. I even got a gerbil. Nothing seemed to work.

Or maybe everything did because in ninth grade, my life suddenly changed. The anxiety I felt every minute of the day and night finally dissipated. In fact, I felt great! I decided to go to a large public school. My class size went from 18 in eighth grade to 397 freshman year. I loved my new school. I made new friends. I had a new learning environment with new teachers. I was a new me. Life was good. I joined the student council. I got straight-A grades effortlessly where my peers were struggling. I was carefree and felt like nothing could stop me. And nothing did, until after spring break, when my anxiety suddenly returned with a voracious roar.

In English class, my mind never settled down. I kept thinking about illnesses even though I liked to read. In Geometry, I would constantly feel worried but often not know why even though math was a favorite subject. In Biology, I thought about threats to my own safety, my friends' and family's safety, or the safety of others that I didn't even know even though science was very interesting. My anxiety had always been a shape-shifter, but it was much less amorphous than it had been when I was younger. It got so bad that my anxiety would cause me to visibly shake at just the thought of having to leave my mom to go to school. When I started having difficulty simply leaving my house without crying my world began to rapidly shrink. Gone went rock climbing because being up high on the wall made me too worried. Gone went friends because I didn't want to be around people. Gone went playing an instrument because I would have to play the piece perfectly and if I made a mistake I'd have to play it over again from the start. Everything was exhausting.

I was miserable. Still, no one was able to really help

me. So, I guess I figured out something that did help me in the moments of pure fear. In order to calm down at home, I started to perform certain rituals. I had no idea why but doing them made me feel better. The acts were random and intermittent. Sometimes I would click the light switch five times, or take the stairs two at a time, or tap my fork twice. But I had no idea why. Then the things that I had to do would change. I'd have to write my homework in perfectly uniform letters or else I would have to do the assignment over again. I couldn't have any specks or differentiations in my food or I wouldn't be able to eat it. I needed to wear the same color of shorts every day. But I had no idea why. Then the things that I had to do would change again. I began repeating certain phrases like they were songs stuck in my head. I had to get the last touch if someone touched me. I needed to spin in my chair. I wanted constant reassurance. But I had no idea why. I never stopped worrying about getting sick at school. I felt lost and alone, still anxious and very upset. I began missing school on some school days because it was just too hard for me to be there.

I had always loved learning and really hated not being in the classroom. I knew missing too much school was not an option and I didn't want it to be. I wanted to change. I wanted to have the peace of not worrying about every little thing. I knew I had to try something new, but I didn't know how. I just couldn't stop feeling anxious. After many, many, many, weeks I finally got up the courage to talk to the social worker at my high school about an anxiety group she was starting. It was hard to describe to her what I was feeling. Not only was it difficult to articulate my feelings of anxiety, it was also hard to share those emotions with someone I didn't really know. I remember her being very practical and making me feel like I wasn't abnormal. She talked with me that first day about creating a safe space. She told me that I could always come to her office and sit in the purple chair. Somehow that helped. She also talked with me about anxiety and OCD. She put a name to what I was feeling. My life slowly began to get a little bit better.

And then just as quickly it didn't. I started having panic attacks at school. During one of my panics, I came to see the social worker. I just sat in that purple chair for a long time. She decided we would work together to laminate notecards with different phrases on them that I could carry with me and look at whenever I felt panicked. They were positive statements to make me realize that I had control over my anxiety. Things like: "I can talk to Mom," "I can talk to Dad." She also told me that jokes sometimes help calm people down. "What did the zero say to the eight?" she asked. "Nice belt!" she smiled and added that one to the pile as well. She even shared with me about how she overcame her personal fears by learning to retrain her mind. I never would have imagined that she had also suffered from unwanted thoughts just like me.

My life started to improve again. Although I felt like I was on a path with a lot of potholes I kept bumping along. I also began seeing a therapist who specialized in OCD and anxiety. What a difference it made! He instantly knew what I was feeling. He instantly knew how I was suffering. He instantly understood how difficult it is to face your fears.

Together we began to dissect OCD and my anxiety. We made diagrams and formulas and talked about my fears in a way that allowed me to gradually get some control over them. It was not easy. I'd have to sit with my anxiety. It was not fun. It took a long time, but I didn't give up. We worked on eating away from the home. I remember how joyous it felt to eat a tiny bite of a granola bar, the size of a half of a raisin, in his office for the first time! We worked on talking with strangers. We worked on not having to rewrite or retype something because it was not perfect. We worked on so many life-skills that come naturally to most people but paralyzed me into a frozen statue. I figured out how to best use cognitive behavior therapy, specifically exposure and response prevention (which my dad calls "face your fears and they will disappear"). We talked and talked and talked.

I don't see him anymore, but I am so grateful for his expertise and support during some of the most difficult periods of my life. I still have those notecards I made with the social worker a few years ago. They are stashed on a shelf that holds all of the items I had used to manage my OCD during that time: the notecards, the multi-colored juggling ball to squeeze if I felt anxious, the mittens. Seeing them reminds me that I can separate my life into pre-OCD, OCD, and post-OCD, where I am right now. Seeing them reminds me that OCD is a battle that is really never over. Thinking back to how I felt during all of those years I'm surprised I even survived it.

When I talk with students at my school, through blog posts, or at other speaking events, people always ask me why I wrote this book. I have two reasons, both equally important. One reason is to educate all individuals about OCD, even people who might have it. Until I had a proper diagnosis, I floundered. I didn't know what was happening to me. Now looking back everything makes sense, but while it was ongoing, nothing did.

A quick computer search reveals that anxiety disorders are the most common mental health disorders in the United States. OCD specifically affects one in 100 people in the United States and one in 200 children. It is about as common as childhood diabetes. I would bet that most people know what diabetes is and how to treat it. Why don't people know more about OCD? Why when people are asked about OCD do they assume it is simply about being clean or tidy or a perfectionist. Why do people associate OCD with positive traits? Why do people who have OCD feel shame or embarrassment to talk about their symptoms? Why does most OCD go undiagnosed or untreated? These are the questions I grappled with when I thought about writing my book.

My second reason for writing this book is to help those who have OCD feel like they are not alone. I wasn't comfortable sharing my compulsions with my therapist or with other teens in my anxiety group. I wasn't comfortable joining a group chat online and talking to strangers that I would never see again about my deepest fears. I was hesitant to even share some of my worries with my brother. So, it makes sense to me that most OCD goes undiagnosed and untreated. What would have been helpful for me was to feel a connection to people who were going through the same thing that I struggle with. Too often books are about the path to recovery; the person is already better. I wanted the immediacy of how hard it is to face OCD every day.

Knowing how hesitant I was to reveal anything different about myself I figured it would be difficult to get people I didn't even know to share their most intimate secrets. OCD can make a person feel ashamed. I decided to use a survey on the Internet that would be anonymous.

I posted it and hoped for a few responses. I was overwhelmed by the number of responses I received. People of all ages, from all over the world completed the survey. The stories I chose to include are moving and meaningful to me as I hope they will be to you. For those who completed the survey and whose stories are not included please know that it does not make your story any less valid.

OCD is a short acronym for something that is so broad and affects so many that it needs some examples. I want this book to provide a platform for people's unique stories to be heard. I believe that if people read this collection of first-hand accounts, and understand how diverse, as well as debilitating OCD can be, then maybe we can change the image of OCD, that it is not just about cleaning, or being well-organized. I want to change the belief that mental illness only affects certain kinds of people — because it affects all of us, at one point or another, directly or indirectly. I want to educate and demonstrate that OCD is debilitating because it is real, just like diabetes, yet so many of the stories share a common theme — one of confusion. The respondents didn't know what was happening to them. I never want anyone else to have to feel isolated like I did. I know there is a strong need to bring these mental health issues out in the open. No one should feel ashamed. It is incumbent upon us to change the mental health narrative.

I believe that advocacy is a good place to start. When I was confused I turned to the Internet. There is a lot of information to sort through about OCD. I found that the International OCD Foundation (IOCDF) was a complete resource. It isn't just a website. It is a well-respected nonprofit organization. The last chapter of this book has valuable information about all of the different resources that the IOCDF provides. Since the IOCDF helped me in so many ways, I decided that fundraising for the IOCDF is a perfect way to start changing misconceptions about OCD. All proceeds from the sale of *OCD to Me: An Anthology of Anxieties* will be donated to the IOCDF in order to help to broaden awareness and provide support to the OCD and related disorders community.

There are all kinds of ways to advocate. A parent can advocate for a child. An individual can speak out about an established cause in a variety of ways, such as holding meetings or using the Internet. Someone can raise awareness about something that matters to that person by starting their own cause. I chose to write a book and use that platform. But advocacy can also mean self-advocacy. What I mean by self-advocacy is be courageous. I know that it is easier said than done. In these pages you will find information about OCD, tips to manage OCD, and thoughts about how to make a difference. Every person is different. I hope people who read this book will be inspired to find their path.

Here are a few things that have worked for me.

1. I made a list of statements that expressed how I felt and that I wanted my friends and family to know about anxiety:

    a. I don't want to have anxiety.

    b. Anxiety can strike at any time.

    c. It may seem irrational to you, but my fears are very real to me.

d. Sometimes when I feel anxious I have no idea why.

e. I don't have to be shaking and look pale and be quiet to feel anxious. In fact, most of the time you would never know how anxious I was feeling inside unless I told you.

f. I analyze things constantly. In fact, my mind is never still. It is exhausting.

g. Sometimes my life is really hard, even if it seems to you that things are going well and there is a lot to be happy about.

h. It is hard to focus on tasks at hand when I'm hyper-focused on my anxiety.

2. I tried to be mentally present which is very difficult to do.

3. When I started feeling nervous and the thoughts started to creep into my head I took deep breaths and slowly exhaled.

4. When my anxiety would tell me to do or not do something I would not give in.

5. When anxiety hit I would distract myself. It's hard, but I would look around the room for things that were a certain color, or I would count backwards from 100, or I would get up and move around, or even jog in place, or do a few jumping jacks.

6. Having a support group is really important. This can be a trusted friend, a family member, a loved one, or an anxiety specialist, but true change can only come from within. You can do it!

7. Finally, being kind to myself was challenging but it is also really important. There will be setbacks but celebrate even the smallest step forward.

I am just beginning my journey as a youth advocate for OCD and I have met some amazing people from all over the world who have supported me. I hope this book will help raise awareness and strengthen our community.

Chapter Two: Understanding OCD

James Claiborn, Ph.D.

In this Chapter I will provide some basic facts about OCD. I often remark that OCD is a well named disorder. People who have OCD have obsessions and compulsions. Obsessions are defined as intrusive, unwanted upsetting thoughts, images or impulses. They are often seen as foreign to the individual, and as something you would least like to think about. Obsessions may range in content to include almost anything people can think about and sometimes seem quite senseless.

Other times the content of obsessions may be seen as disgusting or horrible. This definition is different from what people often mean when they talk about obsessions or being obsessed. We have all heard about someone being obsessed with another person or an activity. However, what is being described is something the person is focused on and wants to think about. That is not what we mean when we talk about obsessions. Compulsions are behaviors a person engages in to try to stop experiencing an obsessive thought or reduce the distress, usually anxiety, associated with having the thought. This may include both overt behavior and mental behavior. Often the compulsive behavior seems to be clearly connected to the obsession, but it is not unusual for people to have compulsions that seem unrelated to the content of the obsession. The individual may not be able to explain why they feel driven to do the particular behavior or how it is going to help with their fear.

Let me provide some examples. A patient of mine feared she would get HIV/AIDS from germs found on many ordinary surfaces such as furniture or door knobs. She had the obsessive thought that she had contacted something that was contaminated with those germs and she would get AIDS and die, or even worse she would spread it to her family. In response to these obsessions she would engage in compulsive behaviors that were designed to prevent events she feared and help her stop thinking about them. Her compulsions focused primarily on washing and decontaminating. She would wash following a very detailed ritual and use bleach on her hands and household surfaces. She also engaged in avoidance behaviors. While avoidance is technically not a compulsion, it serves the same purpose and we routinely find both in people with OCD. In this example we can see some connection between the fear of getting a disease and efforts to prevent it by washing and using bleach. In a second example, I had a patient who had obsessive thoughts that something bad, such as having a car accident or dying, would happen to a member of her family. She felt driven to carry out mental compulsions involving letters, numbers and road signs. Whenever she was away from home she would look at road signs, and convert the letters on the sign into numbers, such as a=1 and b=2. Next, she would add the numbers from a sign in her head and see if it came out a "good" or "bad" number. If the sum was a good number she could relax but if it was what she considered a bad number she had to find a way to insert a letter in the sign that would make sense, add the number for that letter to her sum for the sign and get the sum to be a good number. She explained that if she didn't do this ritual something bad would happen to a family member and she would be responsible. She could not explain how this manipulation of letters and numbers was supposed to prevent bad things from happening.

Some researchers have tried to classify obsessions and compulsions and when talking about OCD, people often refer to subtypes based on classification schemes. Some types of obsessions and compulsions are more common and may be easily described. The most common type of obsessions may be referred to as contamination and harm thoughts. The most common compulsions may include washing and checking. There is no official list of types of obsessions or compulsions and it is often easy to argue that a particular example might fit in more than one category. When people talk about their OCD they may classify it, or even use an abbreviation to describe it. Because these abbreviations are not standardized this often leads to confusion. I have had people ask me about HOCD, but I have to ask if they mean homosexual OCD or harm OCD, or something else. There is one subtype of OCD that has a commonly used name that leads to even more confusion. That is what is called Pure O. This term is meant to describe having only obsessions and no compulsions. Sometimes people use the term when they are confusing mental compulsions with obsessions. Other times people may not recognize behaviors as compulsions or primarily engage in neutralizing behaviors, which while formally are not compulsions they serve the same function. The biggest problem with describing someone as having Pure O, is that it may lead to missing the compulsions. Recognizing the compulsions and dealing with them is an important part of effective treatment.

How Common is OCD

Experts believe OCD is one of the more common

mental disorders. Some estimate it is about fourth in terms of frequency. Lifetime incidence of OCD is estimated to be roughly 2.3% meaning somewhere between two to three people out of every hundred will develop OCD at some point in their life. It is what I call an equal opportunity disorder, in that it effects males and females at about the same rate, something that is not true for many mental disorders, and it is found all over the world at about the same frequency. OCD often first appears early in life and can be diagnosed even in young children. Boys tend to develop it at an earlier age than girls but as they get older the girls catch up. If a person is going to develop OCD they will usually do so by early adult years. It is unusual for people to develop OCD after their 30s, but it has been reported. It may take many years before OCD is recognized and when an older person seeks treatment for the first time, a careful history will often reveal that they have had OCD much of their life.

OCD tends to be a chronic disorder. This means that once someone develops the disorder they are likely to always have some symptoms. Even individuals who never get treatment may report that their symptoms change over time. Some individuals report long periods of time when the OCD is not bothering them, followed by the OCD becoming more severe again.

Some people will describe changes in severity of their OCD and associate it with events in their lives, but others will not be able to identify any explanation. Some women report significant changes, or first appearance of OCD symptoms associated with pregnancy and reports of changes in OCD symptoms are sometimes associated with a woman's menstrual cycle.

What Causes OCD

The easy answer is we don't know. If we go back in the past, Freud thought OCD was caused by particular experiences early in childhood. Modern models include a genetic contribution. It is likely that there are several genes that may lead to a person having a predisposition to develop OCD. Some events during development may then switch on this potential. We know that OCD tends to show up in families and yet there are identical twins who have the same genes but only one develops OCD. One cause for OCD may be an autoimmune disorder. In what is known as PANDAS (pediatric autoimmune neuropsychiatric disorders associated with streptococcus) a reaction to a strep infection may lead to the body's immune system attacking part of the brain. Children who have PANDAS may go to bed normal and wake up with severe OCD. If PANDAS is recognized it may respond to treatments that directly address the strep infection and autoimmune response. However, once well-established, the OCD will probably need to be treated the same way as any other case of OCD.

Similar problems may occur with other diseases, a condition called PANS. PANDAS and PANS are believed to be rare and not the cause of most cases of OCD. People often ask if OCD is related to trauma and there are some cases of people who have developed OCD following a trauma who don't appear to have indicators of genetic risk such as family members with OCD. However, most people with OCD don't have evidence of a clear relationship between trauma and developing OCD. Research has identified some differences in brain functioning in people with OCD and these differences help understand what is happening in the brain in people with OCD. There is also evidence that treatment with CBT and medication both may produce changes in brain function so that it resembles function of people who don't have OCD.

How is OCD Diagnosed

Like mental disorders in general there is no specific medical or psychological test to diagnose OCD. In practice the diagnosis is made based on interview and observation. Adults and teens can usually describe the thoughts that constitute obsessions although they may be reluctant to talk about them. They may also recognize that some of their behaviors are compulsions. The diagnosis is made if the person has obsessions and/or compulsions that take up a significant amount of time and cause significant interference with function or distress. Making the diagnosis in children is more difficult. Many children may find it difficult to describe their experience or recognize that it is not normal. Some features of normal child behavior such as wanting to repeat a behavior or unusual fears may be part of normal development. Severity of OCD may be assessed using a scale such as the Yale-Brown Obsessive-Compulsive Scale or YBOCS. This scale asks about time taken, distress, interference and control of OCD.

Chapter Three: Treatment Options

James Claiborn, Ph.D.

In this Chapter I will describe the treatment options for OCD. I will include those that are considered places to start and also some information about unusual options, special cases and what to do when it seems like nothing is working. I will include some ideas about how to look for treatment, questions to ask of a potential treatment provider and some things to look out for that may be red flags.

The treatments recommended here are evidence based so I need to begin by explaining what that means and why it is important. Historically, health care has been provided by people who were trained in a sort of apprentice model. They are medical doctors, psychologists, therapists and others who were trained by people who taught them what they had been taught. Practices and approaches were handed down. Sometimes a new idea or approach would be developed and the person who developed it might get a following or teach students a new approach, but the choices of treatments were not for the most part carefully evaluated. Things began to change in the 20th century as a scientific approach began to take hold. More and more there is an expectancy that health care will be evidence based. This term is given different definitions and I am not going to discuss the debate but suggest the best interpretation is that treatment is evidence based if it has been tested and shown to actually work using the scientific method. To do this we need to carefully define what is involved in the treatment, and carefully measure its effects. It is not good enough to say

I am professor Smartstuff and I know what works.

One of the reasons this is very important is that there are lots of treatments that may be offered to people with OCD that are not evidence based. The source offering the treatment may say I tried it on some people and I think it was great, but those impressions and opinions don't amount to evidence. There is a saying in science that the plural of anecdote is not evidence. In mental health practice today, many providers will offer treatments that have not been carefully tested scientifically. They may claim they have seen it be very helpful but have only their opinion to support that claim. People with OCD are often suffering and desperate to find help. If they spend their time and use up valuable resources seeking treatment that is unproven, they risk not only wasting time and money, but they may actually get worse. It also represents a delay in getting potentially effective treatment. The IOCDF is committed to evidence-based treatment for OCD and encourages research, and training in these approaches.

Medications

The first category of treatments I will discuss is medications. Medication treatment of OCD is the most readily available and most likely to be the first treatment offered. Medications used to treat OCD can be prescribed by many different professionals including primary care providers such as your family doctor or nurse practitioner. They may also be prescribed by a specialist such as a psychiatrist. The most commonly used medications are now well known to most prescribing professionals, but non-specialists may not know the best way to use these medications.

The most commonly used medications used to treat OCD are ones which work on a chemical in your brain called serotonin. Serotonin is one of many chemicals that are used in the brain to send messages from one brain cell to other brain cells. These chemicals are called neurotransmitters. There are probably several neurotransmitters that are important in OCD, but we know that serotonin is one of them. The first line medications used to treat OCD work by blocking reuptake of serotonin. This is a process where the cell that sent out the messenger chemical picks it back up to use later. This process is called reuptake. The first line drugs are all serotonin reuptake inhibitors or SRIs. Some work selectively on serotonin and not other neurotransmitters and are referred to as selective serotonin reuptake inhibitors or SSRIs. Some work primarily on serotonin and on other neurotransmitters and are called SNRIs. All of these medications are considered antidepressants. While all the first line medications used to treat OCD are antidepressants, not all antidepressants are first line drugs to treat OCD.

When these medications are used to treat OCD, they are often used in a way that is different from when they are used to treat depression. Prescribers who are not familiar with treating OCD may not be aware of the differences and this may lead to people getting less effective treatment. When treating OCD, a knowledgeable prescriber will often want to prescribe a high dosage of an SRI. This may mean going up to the maximum recommended dosage for the particular medication and sometimes even more than the maximum. Secondly, it often takes a long time before the effect of the medication is clear. Experts recommend allowing a three-month trial of a particular medication before moving on to another. Although all the first line medications are working by the same mechanism some people will find they respond well to one and not another. The prescribing professional may need to try a series of different medications, taking time to get up to a high dosage and then waiting long enough to see if it will have a beneficial effect. After going through careful trials of the first line medications about 75% of people with OCD will get an important benefit from medication treatment. Research reports suggest that this benefit may average a 30-40% reduction in severity using a standard scale. Some people will get larger benefits, and some will not see much benefit at all.

It is also important to understand that medication treatment only works while the person continues to take the medication. Research shows that if a person stops medication it usually takes about three months before they are back to where they started in terms of symptom severity. People often ask, "what is the best medication for OCD", or "what is the best medication for my type of OCD". The answer is that we don't have a best medication and can't really say one works better than the others. Individuals differ in their response to medication and in the side effects they experience. The best choice for any one person is something you have to work out with your prescribing professional.

When first line treatments don't work as well as we would like, the prescribing professional can try adding other medications using what are called augmentation strategies. This can include using medications that are used to treat other mental disorders, and even some medications used to treat completely different neurological disorders. While I won't go into detail here, if you are not getting much help from SRI medications you can ask your prescriber about augmentation. Since researchers are actively working on finding new ways to treat OCD, the prescriber may want to look at articles on the IOCDF web page that discuss the latest developments.

Cognitive Behavioral Therapy

The next type of treatment I will discuss is referred to as Cognitive Behavioral Therapy or CBT. There are several different things included in CBT and I will describe the major types. CBT is harder to find than medications and is usually provided by mental health professionals who may have different credentials. CBT trained therapists include psychologists, social workers, to other types of professional counselors. Unfortunately, many mental health professionals are not trained in CBT in general or CBT for OCD specifically. It is important to ask about a therapist's training and approach to treating OCD and I will say more about this later.

CBT is a modern term and represents a combination of traditions in mental health treatment. Those traditions include behavior therapy which largely originated in the 1950s and cognitive therapy which emerged in the 1980s. The developers of these approaches were committed to research and developing treatments that we would now describe as evidence based. It is important to know that the focus on evidence-based treatments continues to today.

The most extensively researched and oldest well-tested approach to CBT for OCD is called Exposure and Ritual (Response) Prevention (ERP). In many ways this approach is considered the gold standard in treatment of OCD and something that almost always should be included in most people's treatment. ERP consists of intentional exposure to the triggers for and/or content of obsessions and voluntary inhibition of the compulsive or avoidant behavior that make up compulsions. Let me give a simple example. Suppose a patient comes to me with obsessions about germs found on door knobs. S/he might say that door knobs may have AIDS viruses on them and touching one may cause them to get AIDS and possibly spread it to their loved ones. The same person is likely to describe compulsions and avoidant behavior related to this obsession. They may try to not touch door knobs and wait for someone else to open the door, they may pull their sleeve down over their hand when they can't avoid touching a door knob and they may wash their hands following special rules after they think they might have come in contact with door knob germs.

If we agree to try to approach this combination of obsession and compulsions with ERP, I might develop a plan to have my patient intentionally start touching door knobs and not engage in any behaviors they use to feel better. In addition, I would probably ask them to spread the germs from their hands to other parts of their body and maybe some of their possessions. I would expect that doing this will cause a spike in their anxiety. I would them ask them to allow themselves to experience the anxiety and not try to get the thought that they are contaminated out of their mind or diminish the risks of getting some terrible disease from touching a door knob. I would ask them to sit with the anxiety and give it a score. After a while I would expect their anxiety to decrease. Before they leave my office, I would work out an agreement about doing homework which would involve their doing ERP on their own.

I can imagine a few different responses as you read this. If the fear I described is close to one you have, I would expect you to think how scary that would be and maybe that you could never do such a thing. You might also think what a big meanie I am and that I must be some kind of sadist. Others might be thinking it is silly to be afraid of door knob germs and that it is much different from the things they obsess about. They may also think there is no way to apply ERP to their fears or it might be unsafe to do so. Let me say I have been doing this kind of work for many years and both my experience and the research show it works well. Second, a well-trained OCD therapist can probably figure out a way to apply it to almost any fear you have.

When we use ERP the person first experiences a spike in anxiety, but it usually decreases after a little time and if they do their homework the particular obsession and compulsion we have targeted will become much less of a concern. Notice I didn't say all your anxiety will go away, because it won't, but then again, anxiety is a normal part of human experience. What does happen is the person can go through life without having to spend a lot of time on obsessions or compulsions.

In an earlier part of this discussion of treatment I talked about how effective medications can be. When it comes to CBT, we can ask the same questions. Research and experience suggest that almost 90% of people who get a careful trial of CBT will show important benefits. The benefit may be as much as a 75% reduction in symptom severity using a standard scale. To be fair, these estimates are based on people who complete treatment and who do all the hard homework we ask for. As you have seen, the things asked in ERP are scary and difficult to do. Some people drop out or don't do their homework. Sometimes, therapists may not ask the right questions and design ERP that doesn't work. Just like medication, if you don't take it, or in the case of CBT you don't do the hard work it won't be much help.

There is also research on what happens after people finish CBT. Follow up research like this is difficult and expensive so there is not a lot of it. However, the existing research finds that the benefits of CBT last for years after a person finishes therapy. Some people will continue to improve, some stay about the same and some may get worse. The long-term benefit of CBT depends on the person continuing to apply what they have learned. In my experience sometimes, my patients will come back for booster sessions when a new problem develops, or they need help getting back on track.

ERP is considered the gold standard form of CBT for OCD. This is because it was the first approach shown to work and has the most extensive body of research supporting it. Next, I will discuss other forms of CBT that can be used with OCD.

Cognitive approaches to treating OCD are derived from models of cognitive therapy which focus on thoughts. The basic idea behind cognitive therapies is that it is not what happens to us that upsets us, it is what we think about what happened. A psychiatrist, Aaron Beck, developed a new approach to therapy he called Cognitive Therapy as a way of treating depression. His model has since been expanded to treat a range of disorders including OCD. Research has found that cognitive therapy, using Beck's model is no less effective than

ERP. Other variations of cognitive approaches have developed, including Acceptance and Commitment Therapy (ACT), and Metacognitive Therapy. These newer approaches are less extensively researched but the evidence is accumulating that they are effective treatments. Most modern well-trained CBT therapists will incorporate some aspects of the newer approaches including looking at addressing thoughts, what we think about them and mindfulness.

What to look for

When looking for treatment there are some things to consider and questions to ask. If you are looking for medication treatment, you want to ask the provider about their experience with OCD. While a primary care provider may be the most accessible, they may not be well informed about treating OCD. If they do provide treatment and it is not achieving desired results you can consider going to a specialist such as a psychiatrist.

It is even more important to select a therapist who will offer effective treatment. It is important to ask about their experience treating OCD, and the approach they use. You can ask about training or supervision they have that focused on treating OCD. The IOCDF offers specialized training for therapists, you can ask if they have attended that type of training. Ask specifically about ERP. If the potential therapist doesn't know what this is then it is time to look elsewhere. Another red flag is if a therapist says they need to get to deeper issues to find the cause of your OCD.

When Treatment Doesn't Work

Unfortunately, no treatment works for everyone. In the discussion of evidence-based treatments I gave some estimates of how well the treatments work for OCD. What can you do if you find you have tried the treatments described here and nothing seems to help? There are some choices you can consider. If you have only been treated with medication add CBT. There is solid evidence that this will usually lead to improvement. Similarly, if you have only tried CBT, adding medication may help. If you have been working with someone who has limited experience treating OCD consider trying to locate someone with more expertise.

Another option is to consider more intensive treatment. Many people seeking therapy will see their therapist for about one hour a week. It may be that more hours or specialized intensive treatment will make a big difference. This includes the options of intensive outpatient treatment programs and residential treatment. There are a number of centers around the U.S. that offer intensive outpatient treatment for OCD and a few places that offer residential treatment. The IOCDF website is a great source for information about specialized treatment centers.

For the unfortunate individuals who do not respond to treatment including intensive residential treatment and trials of alternative medications there may still be options. These include some forms of neurosurgery including implanting a brain stimulating computer chip. These treatments are reserved for people who have very severe OCD and who have not been able to benefit from traditional treatments.

Chapter Four: Disorders Related to and Sometimes Confused with OCD

One of the stumbling blocks to accessing effective treatment for individuals with OCD is that OCD can sometimes be confused with other disorders. The newest edition of the *Diagnostic and Statistical Manual of Mental Disorders (DSM-5)* — which mental health professionals use to help diagnose mental health disorders — in fact, groups together these "related disorders" in the same chapter. While some disorders can have overlapping symptoms with each other, being diagnosed with the right disorder has incredibly important implications for treatment, and therefore it is important to make sure you receive the right diagnosis. For example, a sprained ankle is treated differently than a broken ankle. Even similar disorders can have very different treatments. And providing the wrong treatment for someone can result in extended, unnecessary suffering, wasted time, wasted resources, and potentially feeling hopeless about getting better.

Below is a list of disorders grouped together in a "chapter" in the *DSM-5* because they share some common characteristics but can also be differentiated in predictable ways. These are all referred to as Obsessive Compulsive Related Disorders or OC Related Disorders (they are also sometimes called OC Spectrum Disorders):

Related Disorder	How This Disorder "Looks Like" OCD	How This Disorder Differs from OCD
Hoarding Disorder To learn more: Visit the IOCDF Hoarding Center Website.	"Compulsive Collecting" has up until recently been considered a sub type of OCD. **People with Hoarding Disorder and people with OCD both:** May spend a great deal of time preoccupied with arranging, ordering and/or collecting items.	**People with Hoarding Disorder:** Don't see a problem with their excessive collecting. Don't respond well to traditional OCD treatments such as Exposure and Response Prevention (ERP) or anxiety-based treatment approaches. **People with OCD:** Don't want to engage in their compulsive behavior. Don't get any pleasure from saving things and the resulting clutter, which they find to be unwanted and highly distressing. Have few sentimental attachments or beliefs about the value/worth of the items themselves.
Body Dysmorphic Disorder (BDD) To learn more: Download the BDD Fact Sheet. Visit the IOCDF's Help for BDD Website	**People with BDD and people with OCD both:** Do repetitive checking.	**People with BDD:** Have checking behaviors and obsessions that only focus on their body or the way they look. Are very likely to seek cosmetic surgery. **People with OCD:** Do not usually have thoughts or behaviors that focus on the way they look.

Body Focused Repetitive Behaviors (BFRBs) (Trichotillomania / Hair-Pulling Disorder And Skin-Picking / Dermotillomania / Excoriation Disorder) To learn more: Download the Trichotillomania Fact Sheet. Visit TLC Website.	**People with BFRBs and people with OCD both:** Do repetitive behaviors. Do repetitive behaviors in response to feeling uncomfortable.	**People with BFRBs:** Get a good feeling from pulling out their body hair or picking at skin; some use it to relieve stress. Respond better to habit reversal and to different medicines then people with OCD. **People with OCD:** Repeat their behaviors to get away from bad feelings like anxiety.
Olfactory Reference Syndrome (ORS) To learn more: Read "What Is Olfactory Reference Syndrome (ORS)?"	**People with ORS and people with OCD both:** Have obsessions that cause them distress. Perform repetitive behaviors to try and get rid of the distress caused by their obsessions.	**People with ORS:** Only have obsessions about their body odor/the way they smell. **People with OCD:** Can have obsessions related to a wide variety of topics.

In 1998, Dr. Susan Swedo identified a subtype of OCD in kids which she referred to as PANDAS. The importance of this observation is that these children tend to show OCD symptoms in a more extreme way and need medical attention in addition to psychological help. It is important, in cases where a child shows OCD symptoms "seemingly overnight" and with a severe onset, that they be evaluated by their pediatrician as soon as possible.

Related Disorder	How This Disorder "Looks Like" OCD	How This Disorder Differs from OCD
Pandas / Pans (Pediatric Autoimmune Neuropsychiatric Disorders Associated With Streptococcal Infections) / (Pediatric Acute-Onset Neuropsychiatric Syndrome) To learn more: Visit the IOCDF's OCD in Kids Website.	**Children and teens with OCD and PANDAS/PANS both:** Experience typical obsessions (fear of contamination; fear of harm; over responsibility, etc.) Experience common compulsions (excessive checking, washing and/or cleaning, or reassurance seeking, etc.)	**Children with OCD:** Typically see first onset between 8–12 years old, and symptoms become gradually more severe over time. **While PANDAS/PANS:** Typically affects children between 4–14 years old, with acute (sudden), dramatic onset of symptoms. Additionally, children with PANDAS/PANS will show additional symptoms not typically seen in kids with OCD including: Severe separation anxiety. Anorexia or disordered eating. Urinary frequency. Tics and/or purposeless motor movements. Acute handwriting difficulty.

In addition to the Related Disorders there are some additional disorders that are commonly confused with OCD. These disorders show some common characteristics and overlapping features but can also be distinguished from OCD and one another by a well-trained mental health provider. These disorders include:

Similar Disorder	How This Disorder "Looks Like" OCD	How This Disorder Differs from OCD
Tic Disorders/Tourette Syndrome To learn more: Read the Expert Opinion on OCD and Tourette Syndrome. Download the Tourette's Fact Sheet. Visit the Tourette Syndrome Association Website.	**People with Tics/ Tourette Syndrome and people with OCD both:** Repeat physical behaviors like eye-blinking, touching or tapping. Repeat vocal behaviors like clearing their throat.	**People with Tics or Tourette Syndrome:** Do their tics because they have a sense of discomfort or need to feel "just right". Respond better to habit reversal and to different medicines than people with OCD. **People with OCD:** Do their repetitive behaviors in response to an obsession (thought or image).

Impulse Control Disorders (Addictions To Gambling, Sexual Activity, Excessive Shopping) To learn more: Visit the Treatment 4 Addiction Website.	**People with Impulse Control Disorders and people with OCD both may have:** Strong urges to repeat certain behaviors Attention problems.	**People with Impulse Control Disorders:** Repeat their behaviors as a way to increase good feelings like arousal or excitement and engage in risky behaviors. **People with OCD:** Repeat their behaviors to get away from bad feelings like anxiety and tend to go out of their way to avoid risk.
Obsessive Compulsive Personality Disorder (OCPD) To learn more: Download the OCPD Fact Sheet.	**People with OCPD and people with OCD both have problems with:** Making excessive lists: Perfectionism.	**People with OCPD:** Have problems finishing tasks because of their preoccupation with perfectionism. Don't see a problem with their "symptoms". **People with OCD:** Do not always have perfectionism problems. Do not like their OCD "symptoms".

Autism Spectrum Disorders To learn more: Read the Expert Opinion on Asperger's and OCD. Visit the Autism Speaks Website.	**People with Autism Spectrum Disorders and people with OCD all may have:** "Stereotyped" behaviors like following rigid routines, an "obsessive" interest in something.	**People with Autism Spectrum Disorders:** Usually have thoughts and behaviors that only focus on repeating things. Don't try to prevent their thoughts. Have severe problems with social interactions. **People with OCD:** Usually have thoughts and behaviors that focus on contamination violent/sexual themes checking, etc. Try to stop their bad thoughts from happening.

Psychotic Disorders/ Schizophrenia	**People with Psychotic Disorders/ Schizophrenia and people with OCD both may have:** Strange or bizarre thoughts. Thoughts that include sexual violent or religious themes.	**People with Psychotic Disorders/Schizophrenia:** Have delusions. Their thoughts aren't based in reality but the person believes the thoughts to be true. **People with OCD:** Usually know that their obsessive thoughts don't make sense even if they respond to them as though they are "true." Can stay in touch with reality in all other areas of their lives.

International OCD Foundation

PO Box 961029, Boston, MA 02196

617.973.5801

Chapter Five: OCD Myths

James Claiborn, Ph.D.

In this Chapter I will identify and discuss some of the myths about OCD. Most myths involve absolute statements. They may include statements like "everyone with OCD" or "people with OCD always". OCD is really a very diverse disorder and generalized or absolute descriptions are likely to be inaccurate.

1. Everyone with OCD is overly neat and organized.

Not at all

While some people have compulsions that involve straightening, ordering or cleaning, there are many people with OCD who are very disorganized, and my not care at all about symmetry or neatness.

2. People with OCD spend lots of time washing their hands.

Kind - true

Hand washing is one of the most common compulsions but not universal. Sometimes people will insist they don't have OCD because they don't have this compulsion.

3. People with OCD are very intelligent.

I like to think so

Sorry but this is also a myth. While some people with OCD are very intelligent, the research shows that IQs of people with OCD are not different from the general population.

4. Having OCD makes you good at detailed jobs.

There is evidence to support the idea that people with OCD pay more attention to details than most people. This may lead to not being able to see the forest for the trees. That is that people with OCD may miss the bigger picture because they are over focused on details. This tendency to over focus is more likely to cause problems than be a big help.

5. Having thoughts about harming people means you are dangerous.

This myth is a big problem and is shared by many people including many people with OCD. I often hear my patients tell me that if they have thoughts of harming someone they are afraid they will do it and afraid to tell anyone because they will get locked up. We have lots of evidence that having this kind of thought is not abnormal or uncommon. These thoughts are upsetting to people because they fear they will do something they don't want to do. There is no evidence that having these thoughts is dangerous or that people with OCD are more (or less) likely than anyone else to harm others.

6. Everyone has a little OCD.

While everyone probably has some intrusive thoughts that are similar to obsessions or may have some behaviors that are similar to compulsions, that is not enough to say they have a little OCD. Many of my patients are upset by people casually saying they have

OCD or saying things like “I am so OCD”. People who have OCD, have a serious disorder, and although it varies in severity, it involves significant distress and interference with function.

7. Everyone with OCD is afraid of germs.

Fear of germs and more general fear of contamination is one of the more common obsessions. However, there are lots of people with OCD who don’t have this type of obsession. Even contamination obsessions are not always about germs. People and places can be seen as contaminated in some way that doesn’t involve the idea of germs. Some people with OCD have what is described as emotional contamination.

8. OCD is caused by bad parenting.

Part of this myth goes back to Freud, who believed that OCD was caused by something going wrong during toilet training. This idea has evolved, and now it is common for people to believe OCD is related to general bad parenting, or some trauma in childhood. As discussed elsewhere, we don’t have a complete explanation of why people develop OCD; genes and environment act together to determine who develops OCD.

9. It is important to understand why you have these thoughts or obsessions.

This is another myth that started with Freud. He believed obsessions represented some unconscious conflict and that getting to the root of this conflict was necessary for treatment. The intrusive thoughts that make up obsessions represent a normal process in which our minds generate thoughts. They become a problem for people with OCD because of how they react to them and give them importance. Trying to figure out why you have these thoughts makes them seem more important and makes OCD worse.

10. You need to stop thinking these horrible things.

As I noted above the thoughts that become obsessions are normal events. They occur involuntarily and can't be controlled. Trying to control them won't work and leads to getting frustrated or upset. If I asked you to not think about polar bears no matter what you would find yourself thinking about them. When we try to suppress thoughts, they become more noticeable.

11. There is a form of OCD with no compulsions called Pure O.

The term Pure O is used to describe a form of OCD where the person shows no overt compulsions. The myth is that these people have no compulsions. People with OCD who think they have Pure O and therapists who think they have it, are making one or both of two common mistakes. The first mistake is confusing mental compulsions with obsessions. Mental compulsions may take the form of repeated review of events to try to be certain about what happened. This includes trying to be sure the door is locked, or the person didn't say or do something inappropriate. The second mistake is not recognizing behaviors that are compulsions such as reissuance seeking or serve the same function as compulsions even if they don't quite meet the formal definition such as avoidance.

12. OCD and OCPD are the same problem.

There are two different disorders with very similar names and many people including mental health professionals confuse them. One is OCD which is described in this book and the other is Obsessive-Compulsive Personality Disorder (OCPD). OCPD is a disorder which involves traits like, being preoccupied with rules, perfectionism, being inflexible or rigid, and being miserly. The diagnostic criteria does not include obsessions or compulsions. While a person can have more than one mental disorder most people with OCD don't have OCPD. The confusion and similarity of names is really a result of older theories that held that the disorders were related.

Chapter Six: Tips for Overcoming OCD

Fred Penzel, Ph.D.

"Every day I wake up and say, 'I have to deal with OCD,' but then I remind myself that OCD has to deal with me."

- An anonymous OCD sufferer

Let's begin by agreeing that one brief section in a book cannot possibly tell you everything you need to know about how to overcome something as complex and devious as OCD. On the other hand, if some of the advice here sets you on the right path or helps you to improve what you are already doing, then it will have accomplished what it was intended to do. Also, not everyone will be reading this advice from the same perspective, and therefore parts of it may not apply to you in particular or may be things you have already learned. Some of you may never have been in treatment, some of you may be seriously considering treatment, some of you may already be in treatment, and some of you may have already completed treatment. Therefore, just take from it what you need. Sometimes one good tip phrased the right way can have an impact that can make all the difference. These tips have been organized as numbered lists to better enable you to locate the ones most important to you.

Tips for Those Not In Treatment or Who Are Considering Treatment:

1. There is much incorrect information out there about OCD treatment. Despite what you may have heard, therapy for OCD is not some kind of torture procedure designed to push you over the edge or make your life miserable. Ultimately, facing your fears is really the best way to overcome them. There is a saying that "Facing your fears is a way of getting closer to the truth." Many OCD sufferers have theories about what will happen if they come into contact with what they fear. Most of these theories tend to be rather extreme. Unfortunately, active sufferers never stay in their feared situations long enough to find out what really happens. They superstitiously believe that their feared consequence didn't happen because they did a compulsion or totally avoided the situation. They then stay trapped in their beliefs. Behavioral therapy helps sufferers break out of this trap by helping them to test their theories. The truth they discover, is that none of the things they fear happening ever come to pass. Gaining this information over and over again disproves their disaster theories, reduces their fear, and increases confidence when facing obsessive thoughts, triggers, and feared situations.

2. OCD is chronic, meaning that you won't simply wake up one morning and find that it has disap-

peared. Although it is true that you can have remissions, don't count on them lasting indefinitely. This is why we don't use the word *cure* when it comes to OCD. You may not want to hear this, but the good news, however, is that you can recover, meaning that you really can get your symptoms under control and live a normal, productive life. Recovery is always possible for anyone willing to do the steady work necessary to achieve it.

3. Carrying out compulsions as you have been doing just doesn't work in the long run. Compulsions are a person's own really bad solutions to dealing with the anxiety caused by obsessive thoughts. They may fool you by appearing to work for a while, but in the end, OCD will overcome them with doubt, and they will not solve anything. You will soon find yourself having more thoughts, doing more compulsions that will now become strong habits that will take work to get under control. Be aware that seeking information and reassurance are actually two types of compulsions. Time will go by in any case, and you would be wise to use it to work towards recovery, rather than trying to get better at avoiding them.

4. Some people mistakenly believe that OCD is making them do compulsions, but actually sufferers train themselves to do compulsions and then practice them repeatedly, turning them into strong habits that become more and more difficult to resist. When you feel compelled to do a compulsion, it is really the pull

of habit that you are sensing. OCD can only tell you things. It cannot *make* you do things. It only has what power you give it.

5. Don't put off getting treatment for some 'perfect' future time when things will be easier in some magical way. Many people say they will get to work on things at some future date, but this is usually just procrastination – a type of avoidance people practice when faced with things that make them anxious. Often, that future date never happens. Meanwhile, as you wait for that ideal time, your life is going by and you will continue to suffer. The ideal time to work on recovery is as close to 'now' as possible.

6. Facing your fears will, at first, seem like a big risk. You need to be willing to accept this risk. Remember that all life is risky business. Risk is an integral part of life, and as such, it cannot be separated out. Keep in mind that not recovering is the biggest risk of all. An old saying goes, "Show me someone who isn't taking any risks, and I will show you someone who isn't doing anything." Also, in facing your fears, you come to learn the truth about them – what really happens, versus what you fear is going to happen.

7. In good treatment, you will be a partner in the process. You will work together with your therapist to help plan assignments. Therapy homework will be a gradual process, beginning with lower level things that you can most easily start with and working up to things

that are more challenging. No one forces you to do anything, and if you don't feel ready to do something in a whole step, it may be approached more gradually in smaller steps.

8. Self-help is also possible, but it does require a lot of motivation and determination. If there are no specialists anywhere near you, you may have no choice but to turn to self-help. If you are going this route, at least get expert advice from some of the better OCD self-help books. Be careful about relying on amateur advice on the Internet or from people who mean well but don't really understand the disorder. What they tell you may not be correct or reliable.

9. You need to become indignant with your OCD and the effect it is having on your life. You should question why you have to live according to all the illogical rules it creates for you, when all those other people around you do not. It's not your fault that you have it, and there is no reason why it should be allowed to make many important decisions for you and limit your choices. It is good to develop the belief that you just aren't going to take it anymore and try to prepare yourself to do whatever it takes to regain control.

Tips for Those In Treatment: 

1. With OCD, always expect the unexpected. An intrusive obsessive thought can occur any time and any place. Obsessions often have particular themes. No one knows why a person gets thoughts on a particular theme. These themes can either stay the same or can change without warning. Don't be surprised if this happens. It is typical.

2. Obsessions can be about anything. They are only limited by your imagination. The important thing to understand about them is that the subject matter is irrelevant. This means that we do not look for deep meaning in them or analyze them. There are no answers when it comes to this. Sufferers ask themselves, "What does having such thoughts say about me?" In reality, the thoughts are no kind of reflection on you at all. Also remember that you cannot successfully question them or argue with them. There's really no one there to question or argue with.

3. OCD was once known as "the doubting disease." It can attach doubt to just about anything you can think of, and it can be a type of doubt that just won't quit. Seeking information to relieve the doubt simply won't work. OCD is not a problem of a lack of information. You can have enough information to fill a library and it won't help. Getting some kind of answer may help for a little while, but because the doubt is not the type you can settle once and for all, the answer just

won't stick, and you will soon find yourself right back to doubting again. Because of this, it is never a good idea to keep looking up information on OCD or on whatever it is you are having doubts or anxieties about. The availability of information on the Internet has not been a good thing for people with OCD. Good treatment will help you to resist doing this.

4. The same is true of reassurance, whether it is from yourself or others. It just won't last and can only make you worse. No matter how often you reassure yourself, OCD will always find a way to overcome it with even more doubt. Also, asking others the same questions over and over is a bad idea, as it will only create bad feelings and lead to unpleasant situations.

5. Contrary to what many sufferers believe, the problem in OCD is not the anxiety resulting from the thoughts. It is really the compulsions. They are what can take over and paralyze your life, take up hours of your time, and keep you from finding out the truth about the obsessions. Typically, people with OCD don't stay with what they fear long enough to find out if the things the thoughts tell them will really happen. If you think the anxiety is the problem, you will only do more compulsions. If you learn to stop doing the compulsions and stay with what you fear, you will, as I have said, learn the truth behind the thoughts, and then reduce the anxiety.

6. If you do go for professional help, it is highly recommended that you seek treatment from an OCD specialist. A general practitioner is not likely to have the experience and training necessary to get the job done. Hopefully, a good general practitioner will admit that they don't know enough and will refer you to a specialist they work with, or know of, or give you a referral list of specialists. One possibility is that the local therapist working with you can get supervision and advice from a specialist in another location. If no therapist is available near where you live, then you may have to turn to self-help. This can be assisted by some of the better OCD self-help books out there that have been written by experts.

7. In OCD treatment, we do not attempt to analyze the obsessions themselves – what they may mean or why you are having the specific types of thoughts you are having. The content of obsessions is really irrelevant and could be about anything (see Tip #2). OCD seems to have an odd knack for picking topics that will bother you the most. They are what seem to stick. You might think of them as 'synthetic' thoughts that have all the appearance of real thoughts but aren't. Trying to find meaning in obsessions is a waste of time. What really matters is what you do about them, and this is where therapy comes in.

8. The most tried and tested approach to treating OCD is known as Exposure & Response Prevention

(E&RP). It teaches you how to face your fears in a gradual step-by-step way and how to resist doing compulsions. The purpose is to help you to see that if you stay with what you fear and don't try to escape or avoid by using compulsions, the anxiety will gradually decrease. What you find is that eventually the thoughts and situations become boring, and their impact decreases. Over time, the more you resist doing your habitual compulsions, the urge to perform them will also weaken, allowing you to more successfully resist them. What you are doing is increasing your capacity to tolerate what you fear to the point where it no longer has any impact on you.

9. Along with facing the obsessive thoughts, accepting their presence and not avoiding them will also be a great help. Don't waste your time trying to prevent or not think your thoughts. This will only have the opposite effect and lead to thinking more thoughts. Studies have shown that you cannot effectively suppress particular thoughts. The reason for this is that in trying to not think of something, you have to first think about what it is you aren't supposed to think about. As mentioned earlier, by agreeing to let thoughts 'be there,' you can actually build up your tolerance to them to the point where they become boring and do not affect you. Your motto should be, "If you want to think about it less, think about it more."

10. In E&RP, expect the therapist to begin by taking a careful history as well as a complete listing of all

your obsessions and compulsions. This information will then be used to make up what is known as a 'hierarchy.'

This is a listing of all your triggers and fearful situations, and each one is given a number rating – either 0-10 or 0-100. These are then organized from lowest to highest, like a kind of 'fear thermometer,' which allows you and the therapist to be able to tell what to begin working on via therapy homework.

11. You can expect to be assigned homework from this point on. At each session, homework will be reviewed, with some assignments continuing, and others that have been completed, replaced with new ones. Homework can take many forms, including such things as agreeing with particular 'bad' thoughts, writing feared words or phrases, visiting feared locations, doing avoided activities, watching videos or reading articles that trigger you, etc. Another frequently used technique is having you listen several times daily to a series of audio recordings that gradually become more challenging, and which say things designed to bring on a moderate amount of anxiety. Another important type of assignment might be to gradually reduce the habit of doing compulsions, which will help to eliminate urges to carry them out. Some things can't be easily divided up, so you may even need to fully resist doing them from the start. Questioning others and looking for reassurance is also discouraged and phased out. Remember, the goal is to build your tolerance to these things to the point where they no longer affect you. If you don't stay with

what you fear, how can you build up tolerance for it?

12. When first hearing about the E&RP therapy process, many people typically ask questions like, "Won't agreeing with my thoughts make me believe them even more?" or "Won't agreeing that I am going to do negative things actually cause me to do them?" The answer to both of these questions is simply, "No." What really happens is that (see Tip #8) you build up your tolerance to hearing these things and staying with them, and eventually will find them uninteresting.

13. There is a common myth out there that obsessions are somehow harder to treat than compulsions. This is simply not true. Although they are treated gradually, the two are treated differently. If the therapy is well-planned and thought out, there should be no special problems in treating either. Some also say that it is harder to deal with mental compulsions than with physical observable compulsions. Again, this is not true at all. Both can be resisted. Mental compulsions aren't like obsessions, which occur spontaneously and without warning. Mental compulsions are voluntary mental activities that you, yourself, invent and carry out, and as such, can be resisted or disrupted.

14. Remember that dealing with your symptoms is your responsibility alone. Don't involve others in your homework (unless specifically told to) or expect them to push you or to provide the motivation. These

others won't always be there when you need them, but you are always with you, 24/7. The goal is to always manage your OCD independently. The only exception to this is in the case of young children or people with special needs, who may need some assistance in organizing and scheduling their homework.

15. Be prepared to use your therapy tools at any time, and in any place. OCD won't always give you a warning. Also, if new thoughts start to appear, be sure to tell your therapist, to keep them informed.

16. If you get the urge to seek reassurance from yourself or others, you will learn to tell yourself instead, that the worst will happen, is happening, or has already happened. Reassurance will cancel out the effects of any homework you do and prevent you from improving. Reassurance-seeking is a compulsion, no matter how you may try to justify it. It is a form of escape and avoidance. As a safeguard, you can inform those who have been involved in your reassurance-seeking to resist answering questions you may have on certain topics.

17. Try not to get too elaborate when agreeing with obsessions – simply say the thoughts are true and real. Also, do not make fun of, ridicule, or minimize them.

18. Be careful to not ridicule or minimize your obsessive thoughts. This would include not saying such

things as "It's only OCD," or "These thoughts are stupid and meaningless." This is really only another form of reassurance, designed to avoid the anxiety, rather than facing it.

19. Try to not get upset and blame yourself if you slip and do a compulsion. You can always turn it around and do something to cancel it, such as re-exposing yourself. Try to not be a black-and-white all-or-nothing thinker who tells themselves that they are now a total failure. The good news is that you are in this for the long haul, and you *always* get another chance. It is normal to make mistakes when learning new skills, especially in therapy. It happens to everyone now and then. Accept it. Even if you have a good-sized setback, don't let it throw you. Remember the saying, "A lapse is not a relapse." This means that you never really go back to square one. To do that, you would have to forget everything you have learned up to that point, and that really isn't possible. Also remember the saying, "Never confuse a single defeat with a final defeat" (F. Scott Fitzgerald), and as they say in AA, "You can always start your day over."

20. Don't get too impatient with your rate of progress or compare your results with someone else's. Everyone progresses at their own particular rate. Try, instead, to simply focus on carrying out each day's homework, one day at a time and doing the best job that *you* are capable of. You can't do better than your best.

And your best may be different at different times.

21. When you have a choice, always go toward the anxiety, never away from it. Remember - the only way to overcome a fear is to face it. You can't run away from your own thoughts, so you really, in the end, have no choice but to face them. If you want to recover, you will have to do this eventually. Better to do this sooner than later. When faced with two possible choices of what to confront, always choose the more difficult of the two whenever possible.

22. Get your homework in writing, or if you are doing self-help, write it down yourself, either on paper or in your phone. Review your therapy homework assignments daily, even if you think you know all of them. It is easy to overlook and forget them – especially the ones you don't look forward to doing.

23. If your therapist gives you an assignment you don't feel ready to do, don't be shy about saying so. As half of the team, you should be able to have a say in your own therapy. The goal at each step is for the homework to produce moderate anxiety you can get used to tolerating - not to overwhelm you with it and cause you a setback. On the other hand, don't be afraid to stretch yourself a bit whenever you can, and step outside your comfort zone.

24. Procrastination is a feature of many people's OCD, so start your homework assignments the day you

get them. Don't wait for the *perfect moment* to start. The *perfect moment* is whenever you begin doing them.

25. Perfectionism can be another feature of OCD. You may find your OCD telling you that if you don't do your homework perfectly, you won't recover. If you do find yourself obsessing about having to do your homework perfectly, you risk turning it into more compulsions. Some people in these situations are even assigned to agree that they aren't doing things perfectly and won't recover. Watch out for having to do your homework according to the same rigid rules each time you do it. Also, don't do your homework so excessively that it takes up your whole day. Remember that you still have a life to live and things to do.

26. It is important to be aware that OCD may also try to interfere with your treatment. This is very common and not always recognized as a symptom. As mentioned in Tip #25, it can tell you that you aren't doing it correctly and that you will fail. It may also tell you such things as – "You really don't have OCD and are getting the wrong treatment," "You are the exception who won't respond to treatment: "You are just making up your symptoms to get sympathy or to get out of doing things," "You will never understand how to do treatment," etc. Remember that OCD will try to cast doubt on anything that is important to you. To fight this, you may have to agree with these ideas by saying such things as, "Yes, that's right. I really won't get better."

27. Be careful when carrying out assignments to not undo them by telling yourself that "It's only homework, and the things I'm saying and doing don't count and aren't real," or "My therapist wouldn't ask me to do something that would cause harm to me or others," or "I'm only doing this because I was told to, so I'm not responsible for anything bad that happens." This is all just another type of reassurance and will cancel out the assignment you have just done.

28. Try to not let yourself get distracted and *tune out* when doing certain assignments, so that you don't have to feel the anxiety. People sometimes let the homework become routine and do it in a very automatic way as a kind of avoidance. Also, don't do homework while you carry out other distracting activities. Give it your full attention, focus on what you are doing, and let yourself feel the anxiety. To get the full benefit of your homework, you have to be in the moment with it.

29. When faced with a challenging assignment or an unexpected challenging situation, try to look on it as a positive, and as another opportunity to get better instead of saying, "Oh, no. Why do I have to do this?" or "Why did this have to happen?" Tell yourself, "This will be good for me. I need this, and it will be another chance to practice and get even stronger."

30. Try to not rush through your therapy homework so that you don't have to feel as much anxiety.

Take your time and see if you can view it in terms of all the good it will do you. Getting it over with as quickly as possible is not the goal. Raising a moderate level of anxiety and staying with it, is.

31. If your homework doesn't really produce any anxiety, tell your therapist about it. If your exposure homework doesn't cause at least some anxiety, it isn't going to be effective in helping you. On the other hand, try doing all new assignments for at least a week before deciding that they don't make you anxious and won't produce results. Some people may experience delayed reactions and it may take doing an assignment a few times before the anxiety occurs.

32. Never forget that you have OCD. This means that you will not always be able to trust your own reactions or sensations, especially if they seem to be telling you very negative, magical, and extreme things. Often, the anxiety can be your guide. If you are unsure if something *really* is a symptom, treat it as a symptom. Better to err on the side of doing a bit more exposure than not enough.

33. Always take a moment to endorse your own efforts and recognize your successes. It's a good way to help keep up your motivation. Look back at earlier assignments that are no longer challenging if you believe you aren't making progress.

34. Overall, understand that OCD is very para-

doxical. The things that you originally thought would make you better, only made you worse, and the things you thought would make you worse are the very things that will make you better.

35. Medication can be a great help for many sufferers. It should not be regarded as a 'cure' in itself, but instead as something to help you to do therapy. Those with milder forms of OCD may be able to get along without it; however, those with moderate or more severe OCD will find their efforts in facing their symptoms to be a lot more successful with the aid of medication. Medication can lower the frequency of obsessive thoughts and also make them less intense. If a sufferer appears to be struggling with their homework and not making progress as expected, it may be time to bring medication into the picture. Some people have false beliefs about medication. Medication won't give you a new personality, cause you to be some kind of zombie, or create artificial moods, and if properly prescribed should not interfere with your ability to function.

36. Don't underestimate the power of depression and the ways in which it can affect your ability to do therapy. The lack of energy and motivation, and the negativity, in addition to the fatigue which accompany depression can really get in your way. Cognitive therapy can be a big help in dealing with depression. Medication can also be very helpful. Having OCD can certainly be a depressing experience. Many peo-

ple's moods improve as their OCD improves, but if it doesn't, this can be a sign of a separate mood problem that may require treatment. The main thing is to not leave it unrecognized and untreated.

Tips for Those Who Are Post-treatment:

1. As mentioned earlier OCD is a chronic problem, meaning that there is no cure. The good news is that you can make an excellent recovery and have as normal a life as anyone else. Getting well is only 50% of the job. Staying well is the other 50%. Since chronic disorders are not curable, if you achieve recovery, it has to be maintained. This means keeping up some level of maintenance once formal treatment ends.

2. In treatment, you have learned to recognize what your triggers are, and also what to do about them. Even though your former triggers may not now cause you anxiety, it is wise to occasionally challenge yourself with them, to keep up the level of tolerance you gained in therapy. Giving yourself an occasional homework assignment is always a good idea.

3. Even those in recovery may sometimes get an intrusive thought. Intrusive thoughts can even trouble some people without OCD, so expect to have them occur occasionally. In the case of OCD, you have to expect the unexpected. If old or even some new thoughts occur to you, your job is to use the tools you gained in therapy to immediately act on them. Allowing yourself to fall back on old overlearned compulsions to deal with them is a very bad idea and may open the door to more obsessions and compulsions. Remember that compulsions didn't work for you in the past and won't work now. If you face the obsessions without hesitation

and use your therapy tools, you should get them contained in a reasonable period of time. Don't jump to the conclusion that because you are having some renewed thoughts that it proves you cannot recover. This simply isn't true.

4. If you have been getting good results from medication, don't be too quick to stop it as soon as you are feeling better or have recovered. Medications are a control and not a cure. Whatever brain chemistry medication was helping will revert back to the way it was if you discontinue it. In the case of depression, it is generally recommended that people allow themselves to live their recovered lives for about 18 months before attempting to stop medication. This is probably also true in the case of OCD.

5. Symptoms don't always come back immediately after you stop taking your medication. You may notice nothing at first and continue to feel well, which fools some people into thinking that they really didn't need it any more. In reality, it can sometimes take as long as several months for symptoms to reappear. It isn't clear why this may be. If you are determined to discontinue your medication, the best approach is to do it very gradually over several months' time. This way, if symptoms start to creep back in, you will then be able to raise the dosage back up again and prevent a more serious return to previous symptom levels.

6. Many sufferers on medication will end up

continuing on their medication to help them stay recovered. This is simply a fact of life. Many sufferers see medication as a stigma, marking them as 'mentally ill' and 'different' or 'defective' as compared to other people. This simply isn't true. A large proportion of our population takes medication for some chronic condition on a regular basis. If it enables a person to live a normal life and function just the same as everyone else, why should it be regarded as a failure or a mark of shame? Having OCD doesn't represent some kind of weakness or defect. It isn't your fault, and you didn't ask for it. A practical and sensible approach (rather than an emotional one) to dealing with it is much better in the long run.

7. If you find you are having particular difficulties in maintaining your recovery, you should consider going back to your therapist for some 'booster sessions,' or else get back to some more intensive self-help. This should never be seen as a sign of failure but may only indicate you still have some unfinished business to take care of. Such sessions can usually get someone right back on track.

Chapter Seven: OCD Stories from Around the World

Teens

I'm a fourteen-year-old female, and I'm in Middle School. My OCD began to seriously affect my life beginning at the age of twelve. I have Extreme OCD as measured by the Yale-Brown Obsessive-Compulsive Disorder Scale. I focus on contamination and checking. I have mental rituals that involve numbers and counting numbers as well as other mental rituals.

My OCD is like an angry teacher sitting in my head combined with my meanest bully. The bully tells you horrible things to make you hate yourself and the teacher gives you all of these rules that you can't disobey, or they will get very angry at you.

I hope people realize that we aren't beasts or freaks. There is so much more to OCD than the things you can see or the things we let you see.

* * * *

I'm a 12-year-old male. I'm Asian Indian and I was born and live in London, England. My OCD began when I was seven years old. It is mainly checking OCD. I need to ask for reassurance, repeat things a certain number of times, and there also needs to be a certain number of things. I started ERP at age seven. I don't take any medication, but I do take supplements and vitamins to help with anxiety.

OCD is kind of like a voice in your head telling

you to do different things and if you don't do them, you have extreme anxiety. OCD slows you down in everyday things like schoolwork, getting ready in the morning, etc.

My OCD is bossy, and it is harder than you think not to do what OCD tells to do.

* * * *

I am a girl who is 17. I'm a senior in high school and I live in Minnesota. I was recently diagnosed with OCD at the beginning of 2017, after months of dealing with my OCD symptoms and years of dealing with anxiety. I can't remember a time in my life when I wasn't anxious about something. I have harm OCD, and it seems to go hand-in-hand with my depression as well.

My OCD tells me that if I don't harm myself, or take actions towards harming myself, my family will be hurt. What I mean when I say my OCD and depression go hand-in-hand is that if I am in a depressive episode, my OCD gets stronger and harder to resist. If there was a way for you to take a little bit of pain in order to prevent a great deal of pain to the people you love, wouldn't you make that trade? To me, it seems like an easy choice, especially if I am not feeling very worthy, or important, or deserving of love.

I have other obsessions as well, including superstitious OCD, and obsessions about being responsible for causing harm to others indirectly (not giving a homeless person food or money and them dying as a result of my actions), but my main obsessions are violent obsessions of me harming myself, and disturbing intrusive thoughts of ways I could (and should, according to my OCD) hurt myself.

My compulsions include checking, seeking reassurance, avoidance, and scratching. I have been in exposure therapy for my OCD, and I love how it makes me feel in control, not my OCD. I also take medications for my OCD and depression. I have a great treatment team at Rogers Memorial, and I'm proud to say that my current YBOCS scores are in the mild range for OCD. When I began they were in the severe range. I'm currently at a place where I am feeling the best I've felt in a long time, and I no longer feel that my life will be led by my OCD.

OCD is evil. It is manipulative, it preys on your deepest fears, and it tells you that you have to listen to it, or else. OCD makes you feel so small when it is a humongous, terrifying beast. OCD takes your control away from you, and it makes empty promises, "just do this one more time, and then everything will be okay."

OCD does not have to be in control of your life. Having OCD is nothing you need to be ashamed of. You are strong and brave, and you can fight it! Just because you have obsessions does not mean that they are what you want, or what will actually happen. The more you fight OCD, the less power it has over you. Standing up to OCD will be one of the hardest things you'll ever have to do, but it will give you your life back!

* * * *

I am a 17-year-old white female born in Corvallis, Oregon. I sell pottery that I make part- time. I have contamination OCD. I started getting treatment when I was 14. I did solo therapy for two years as well as group therapy at my school. I now do group therapy in Portland and at my high school as well.

My OCD is pretty severe. I have to take a shower if someone touches me and things like that. I had to stop going to school for a while. I went from being an A student to failing all of my classes.

I want people to understand what OCD is like. For me it feels like I'm having the same experience as when you have a crush on someone. It's like a chemical gets released causing you to not be able to stop thinking about them. You become obsessed with them. It's the same with OCD but you are obsessed about almost everything.

I want people to know that OCD really sucks and it's not a joke.

* * * *

I'm an 18-year-old male from Virginia. I'm a student, and I'm single.

I was 15 when I was diagnosed. The doctor's thought it was PANDAS, strep throat that causes OCD, so I had surgeries, but it didn't go away. I was in residential treatment at Rogers, twice, for not eating, fear of throwing up, instructive thoughts, and having trouble leaving the house. Having OCD is an internal struggle every day. It takes everything you enjoy away: from food, to friends, to new experiences.

* * * *

I am a 17-year-old girl. I am a senior in high school and have lived in California my whole life. I was diagnosed with severe OCD when I was 15, but in retrospect I can't think of a time when I didn't have it. I started going to weekly therapy in 9th grade, started medication at the beginning of 10th grade for anxiety and depression, got diagnosed with OCD halfway through 10th grade, and finally went to an OCD specialist the summer before 11th grade. I also found a youth OCD therapy group the summer before 11th grade which helped me make friends and connect with other people with OCD. I am currently in an IOP that I plan to stay in for about 3.5 months. My biggest OCD types are suicide obsessions, sexual obsessions, moral scrupulosity, and perfectionism.

One summer when I was at my grandparents' house I remember lying on the floor in the foot of space between the bed and the wall, urgently whispering confessions to my mom, my phone pressed against my ear. After each confession, I felt a wave of relief, a temporary release, but almost instantly I began to search for the next thing to feel guilty about. It pressed in on my skull and I could feel the next worry there waiting, before I even knew what it was. My heart started racing and guilt flooded me as the thought came to my mind. A bad thought. And then there was the moment when I knew I had to tell her. There was no other way. May as well get it out of the way. After counting down from nineteen I forced it out in a hoarse whisper, waiting for my mom to tell me it was okay. She told me it was normal and not worth worrying about. I told her I couldn't help it. I confessed that I felt the need to confess every bad thought I had. She kind of hinted that I should tell my therapist. No way.

I started frantically trying to stop the worrying. If I didn't I would have to tell a therapist all my embarrassing thoughts and admit something was wrong with me. I knew this wasn't right, but I wasn't sure exactly what the problem was. I tried desperately to just stop thinking about these bad things, but a thought would poke at the outside of my brain and I couldn't help but let it consume me with guilt and fear. I tried the "see it's really nothing to worry about" strategy, which started a vicious internal dialogue, the two parts of my brain arguing about whether or not my thoughts were bad. One part would win, and I would feel a rush of relief, but later the other side would come up with an argument that would take over, flooding my body with guilt again. Confessing went from a building up to a confession every few months to part of my daily schedule. Turn off the lights, count down anxiously from nineteen, confess, and relax. Confessing was once something I thought about for a while debating whether or not to do it. Then I decided that if I just did it without a long wait the relief would come faster.

I started coughing up same-day confessions, even multiple ones per day. The day before a trip I spilled enough confessions to hopefully make it through the whole time I would be away. It often ended up making it worse. The confessions went from something that brought a feeling of freedom and lightness to something that only relieved some of the anxiety, driving me to search my mind for what I was missing. Before, confessing was a one-time thing. Later it began to take multiple tries. Sometimes it would be multiple times in one day. Begging my mom if she was sure it was okay, making her repeat the same consolation multiple times until she seemed worried. Other times I would have time in between before the guilt crept back in and I had to check to see if my mom was sure, maybe even a few times. Overall the confessions started to lose their power. I had to do it more to get the relief. The more frequently I started doing it, the faster the thoughts flowed in and the less satisfaction each confession earned. I became constantly on the edge, waiting for the next thought or debating the last.

I want people to know that it is important to not judge someone's OCD severity based purely on how functional they are. Types of OCD like perfectionism can lead to seemingly good results like exceptional performance in school, but that does not mean that the person is not suffering. Sometimes people assume that others are fine just because they appear okay on the outside, but OCD can be invisible. This was an issue for me because I was convinced that I would die if I didn't get straight A's, which caused me both great distress and success. It was difficult to explain to my parents that I needed to miss some school for therapy even though I was getting better grades than most of my peers in school. It's easy to assume that because you are able to function you don't need or deserve help. I want others to know that that is not true.

* * * *

I'm the mother of a son with OCD. He is 18, white, born and raised in Portland, Oregon. He will be starting college this month.

When my son turned 15, he literally stopped functioning overnight. He was stuck to whatever he touched. He couldn't move, eat, sleep, go to the bathroom, etc. An ambulance came and took him to a psychiatric hospital. They were unable to help him. We got him into an intensive treatment program in LA (Renewed Freedom Center) where he steadily improved. Upon his return home, he began to decline. He finally went to Rogers Memorial Hospital in Wisconsin for four months and lived with other teens suffering from OCD. His OCD involves religious scrupulosity, body dysmorphia, excessive personal cleanliness, intrusive thoughts, difficulty sleeping, and so many more things.

OCD is the inability to go through life in peace. You worry excessively about irrational things. When you finally fight back and stop one behavior, OCD finds another way in and another way to torture you. It's a beast and a bully and it is so misunderstood.

OCD rears its head in times of stress. The transition to college is proving especially challenging for my son. He is smart, friendly, talented and is also tortured, anxious and exhausted.

* * * *

I'm an 18-year-old white female born in Nashville, Tennessee. I'm currently a full-time college student. I have just-right OCD and catastrophizing OCD. I was diagnosed in my junior year of high school. It is serious enough that I work with a therapist regularly, and have coping mechanisms, but though I have considered CBT before, I have never felt I needed it. My OCD typically manifests itself in me obsessing over simple decisions or questions and needing to repeat sensations on my body.

I want people to know that OCD is when you have a thought you cannot stop, called an obsession, and the only way you know how to deal with this is through compulsions, which can really be anything. OCD is not about needing everything to be perfect. OCD can manifest itself in many different ways, and the stereotype of someone with OCD just being a perfectionist is really hurtful. OCD is not your punchline.

* * * *

I'm a 17-year-old Caucasian female from North Carolina. I have had OCD since as long as I can remember. I have Body-Focused Repetitive Behaviors Anxiety, which falls under the umbrella of OCD. It essentially means that I use repetitive motions (often harmful, such as tongue-biting or finger-picking) as a form of self-soothing. I only recently began treatment.

I logically know that I don't have to do these things (and I am a very logic-based person); however, some part of my brain craves these actions, and it reasons with me and nags at me until I do them. It's not a matter of "don't do it," it's a matter of "stop wanting to do it," which is much more difficult.

I want people to know that I'm still a functioning human, and I'm no different than I was before my diagnosis. I think I feel just like anyone else, and I wish they could relate and realize that we're exactly the same: it would feel the same to them if they suddenly felt these urges. Does that make sense?

* * * *

I'm the Mother of a son who was diagnosed with OCD at 17 years of age.

My son has OCD which presents itself in the form of slowness. He was unable to participate in ERP therapy successfully. OCD can be a very debilitating illness. There is so much more to the illness than the common perceptions in our society. OCD affects the individual as well as everyone who loves that person. I admire you for writing this book!

* * * *

I am 18 years old. I was born in India where I currently live. Living in India is difficult if you have mental health problems. India is a conservative culture and it is almost as a "taboo" to speak of your mental health issues here.

I've never seen a doctor since for that I'd have to talk to my family and they will not believe that an 18-year-old has any issues like that. I have obsessions with thoughts and in order to distract myself from them when they get too much I clean. Doing my cleaning takes so much time from life. I clean from the smallest scratch. Every little thing in my house pulls me towards it to clean it.

I feel like I am part of a horror movie that you can't pause. If you want to save yourself, you have to close your eyes and ears, but if you do that you can't live the rest of your life with your eyes and ears closed. When you keep them closed you miss out on your life but if you don't then you have to watch the horror movie.

Nobody really believes it's bad to have this problem. People need to understand that it's not about cleaning. People assume you have OCD and say "Oh! So, you must like to clean." They laugh, and they make jokes, but they don't know what really goes on inside one's head that makes them vulnerable enough to try to do things on repeat. Nobody really asks why so a person with OCD never really wonders why and never realizes their own condition until it gets out of control. I was lucky to study psychology in my high school and learn about mental health but not everyone has that opportunity.

20's and 30's

I'm a single 24-year-old white male born in Grapevine, Texas. I'm a Science teacher.

I have OCD with OSFED and Generalized Anxiety. I was 14 when I first developed OCD. I would describe OCD as an improperly working computer. I want people to know that OCD can be very damaging to life quality and success.

* * * *

I'm a 22-year-old female currently in graduate school to get my Masters of Social Work. I was born in South Carolina and raised in Georgia. I'm dating someone, but I am not married.

OCD started showing its symptoms when I was three or four. I was obsessed with dying or causing my parents to die. I would be terrified of any chemicals and make sure my family knew all the safety precautions for natural disasters. It manifested again when I was 17, and then in my freshman year of college. I started having harm thoughts, sexual thoughts, and religious guilt. Almost everything under the sun. It was a nightmare. I wanted to die because I was so terrified I was going to hurt someone. I self-harmed as a compulsion. I would avoid people. I couldn't eat or sleep. I was a wreck.

Imagine if all your worst fears keep going around in your mind, and the only way you think you can stop them is by doing something repetitive. Only that doesn't work, it only makes it worse. In fact, it makes it so much worse you're trapped. It feels like you're being held at gunpoint, and if you make one wrong move you or someone you love will be shot. It's living in constant fear and dread. It's emotionally and physically draining. I finally found a therapist in Georgia who specializes in OCD and anxiety. I was so relieved when I got a diagnosis. We started CBT and ERP, and it has been extremely difficult. But with medicine and intensive therapy things have gotten better. I have a long way to go, but I'm hopeful for the future.

I am not OCD. I have OCD. I can be successful. I can be in meaningful relationships. OCD doesn't have to win. Fight for yourself. Find a good therapist; don't be scared to try out medication. Therapy is hard, but it's worth it. It may not be fixed overnight, but it does get better. OCD is hell on earth, but you don't have to be stuck there forever, and you're not alone. OCD will try to tell you that you are, but you're not. There is hope.

* * * *

I'm 20 years old. I'm female and I was born and raised in Germany where I am a student.

My OCD began with my pregnancy. I have felt terror ever since. It is indescribable.

* * * *

I am a 23-year-old white male born in Salem, Massachusetts. I grew up in Old Saybrook, Connecticut and currently reside in Middletown, Connecticut. I am in college to get my degree in Music Theory and Composition. I am currently single.

I deal with OCD symptoms related perfectionism,

symmetry, ordering and arranging, touching and tapping, "needing to know," information hoarding, and generally needing things to be "just right." My perfectionism was so severe that I practically lost the ability to read and write; I needed lots of support to graduate from high school and currently use accommodations to get through college. I struggled through residential treatment for OCD because of my co-morbid depression, severe perfectionism and obsessional thinking related to the treatment process. Treatment continues to be a challenge.

Having OCD feels like a set of strict rules your mind forces you to follow. And if you break any of those rules, the consequences may be severe. I also often describe it like walking a tightrope -- you feel like you have to walk an impossibly fine line and you know you're always at danger of falling. But when you decide to set yourself free, you jump off the rope into an abyss of uncertainty. And you learn to live in there and discover it's the only path to freedom.

I want people to know who I truly am outside of my obsessive-compulsive disorder — a musician and student with a passion for mental health advocacy. I want to be known as a caring son, grandson, brother, cousin and nephew. I want people to stop romanticizing OCD as a funny personality trait or an interesting quirk. I want people to know that OCD completely devastates both the individual living with it and their friends and family. And people should know that, at its worst, OCD can take lives.

* * * *

I'm from India. I'm 28 years old. I think OCD started for me at the age of 18. It got progressively worse and now it's really bad. I feel sad and desperate and helpless most of the time. I have contamination OCD. No access to treatment. OCD is not well known in my country and mental health issues are considered taboo. It is very difficult. People think these actions are illogical and crazy.

I would like people to know that OCD is suffering and torture. It's not that I want to perform these compulsions, but I feel compelled to do so.

* * * *

I'm a 37-year-old white female. I was born in Mobile, Alabama, and I still live there. I'm married and a stay-at-home mom. I have had every theme of OCD for most of my life. My symptoms began at the age of eight. When I was 18, my symptoms magnified and became more severe due to intrusive thoughts. I was diagnosed with OCD after the birth of my first child at the age of 21 but was not correctly treated until after the birth of my third child at the age of 33. At this time in my life it was at its worst- for almost a year I couldn't get out of the bed, shower, or eat. I lost 20 pounds in six weeks. After almost two years in treatment I saw some improvement in my mental health. It has been four years now and I can say that I am the healthiest I have been since the age of 18.

OCD is a bully that lives and thrives inside of your brain- spewing lies and causing tremendous turmoil between the irrational and rational parts of your brain. It's a prison inside of your mind and you are held captive. I understand that my thoughts are irrational. Please understand, I know that I am not crazy, but rather the complete opposite, as I know that my brain is not working properly.

After struggling for many years with this disorder, I can say that there is light at the end of the tunnel. For those struggling with OCD know that you will eventually see the difference between who you are and your thoughts. You are not your OCD. Although I know that I will live with this disorder for the rest of my life, I now know how to cope with it, and I hope that others will benefit from hearing my story. Two of my daughters, ages 11, and 15, also have OCD. I am so blessed that I am here to help them though this- as my parents did not know nor did they understand what I was going through.

* * * *

I'm a single, Caucasian female, 22-years-old, born in Springfield, Illinois. I graduated from high school and college, and work as a designer for an architectural firm.

My OCD centers around mental and physical rituals to alleviate fear of failure. The onset came around the age of nine. I remember my symptoms peaked freshman year of college when I found myself unable to leave a public toilet stall due to being paralyzed by fear. I sought treatment at the student health center where they told me to fix myself. I gave up for two more years until my symptoms worsened again. I decided to seek psychiatric help. I take Sertraline daily now. I was going to therapy monthly (until I moved away from college), and I am currently looking for a specialist who treats OCD with cognitive behavioral therapy/exposure response therapy.

OCD is like being trapped in a burning building, while knowing that the door is open. You know it's irrational to feel trapped because it seems like you could escape at any time, but you are afraid that if you leave, something even worse will be waiting for you outside. So, in order to alleviate your fear of the fire (i.e. obsessions), you pour small buckets of water on the closest flames (i.e. performing compulsions). This temporarily helps kill the nearby flames, but they do come back, whether it's in five seconds or five minutes. Other people can see the open door and tell you to come out, but you don't know what's outside of the door, even though you know you should leave. It's nearly impossible to get yourself out the door by yourself, but with the help of others (I.e. Therapists, family, friends), they can come into the house and guide you out. Once out of the burning house, it still takes effort to not run back inside to the "safety" of what is known and what has defined you. It's a constant struggle either way.

What is really difficult is that OCD is not always seen. A person can seem to be extremely happy and successful, and yet can be struggling every day on the inside. Know that this is a real, painful disease, and it should not be joked about or taken lightly. It is not just a "perfection" or "organization" quirk. End the stigma, end the open use of the term "OCD". We are real people struggling and just like everyone else we want to be happy and successful.

* * * *

I am a 22-year-old female who was born in Sacramento, California. I am currently single and am a student. My OCD is mainly Pure O. I have some compulsions, but they are not the stereotypical things such as counting or checking a door.

I had my first panic attack when I was two years old and finally realized something was not right when I was about 10. I was so scared though that I didn't tell anyone. My OCD went into remission from about age 12 to 15. When I turned 16, I started to have symptoms again. I had obsessions that were so disturbing to me at the time that I was in a constant state of anxiety and fear 24/7 for about a year.

I finally reached my breaking point and told my mom and said I needed help because I couldn't "control" my mind and my thoughts and they were making me avoid certain places, people, and things. I went to a psychiatrist and a psychologist for a couple months before starting medication.

Looking back, if I had not gotten help when I did, I don't think I would be here today. I was so scared people would judge me for the things I was thinking. I had such a hard time realizing they were thoughts, not actions and they didn't define who I was. The thoughts scared me, and the fear just fed my OCD even more. I am still on medication and have had a couple relapses throughout college but thankfully I have learned so many tools and have a great psychologist who can help me.

I want people to know that having OCD is not a joke and it isn't just liking to be clean or organized. It's like having another voice in my head that is telling me all these bad things about myself. I know it's not true but eventually I start to believe it because the voice won't stop. It's like my brain is in a constant loop that won't stop. I have to take medication and use other tools to help my brain from getting stuck in that loop. I will tell people it feels like my body is here and present, but my brain isn't. My brain is somewhere else, and it can't escape no matter how much I want it to. OCD is debilitating and a serious illness. It's something I will always have and in a way, it has made me into the kind conscientious person I am today because of the fact that I have become so aware of my mind and its abilities.

* * * *

I'm a 36-year-old, white male. I was born in Silicon Valley and I live in San Diego. I'm single and never married. I have severe OCD. I have had so many OCD symptoms including washing, checking, repeating, ordering, counting, symmetry, perfectionism, and hoarding. However, my dominant obsessions have always been related to eating, vomiting, weight loss, and starvation. I have had these symptoms since age five or six. My parents were very cruel to me about my OCD and didn't understand or care to. I have improved significantly at times when in ERP treatment, but that has been infrequent due to the cost and the inability to find trained therapists covered by my health insurance. I've been on too many meds to count and I don't think any have helped.

OCD severely limits my ability to work (despite great intelligence and the yearning to work) and has limited my social functioning even more severely. I want nothing more than to get sustained treatment, so I could live a more enjoyable and fulfilling life. I am absolutely terrified by things that I rationally know are completely irrational, but that acknowledgement does nothing to reduce the fear. I engage in senseless acts I feel compelled to do in order to provide some temporary anxiety relief, but even more than that I avoid basic life events so that my irrational fears are not triggered. Realizing how irrational it all is does nothing whatsoever to reduce the fear. Only exposing myself to the feared situation without engaging in compulsions reduces my anxiety in the long run, but this therapy causes a tremendous amount of anxiety in the process. It is extremely hard to do and requires incredible courage.

It is nearly impossible to get treatment if you aren't wealthy because there is a shortage of ERP-trained providers. I have "great" health insurance and want to dedicate myself to my treatment more than anything in the world, but I can't afford it because ERP-providers don't accept insurance. The major providers (like Kaiser Permanente) refuse to pay for their therapists to receive ERP training, even while they acknowledge it is the necessary treatment for OCD on their website.

* * * *

I'm 23-years-old. I'm both Italian and French, but I live in Pisa, so consider myself an Italian girl. I'm a student studying archaeology.

I think my OCD started when I was six. I was obsessed with washing hands, then I became afraid of black people. I spent several years washing myself. It ended when I was 14, but unfortunately it started again two years ago. I was afraid to harm myself, then afraid to be lesbian, and right now I am again obsessed with washing myself but mostly my clothes. It's exhausting. I find it difficult because the obsession changes many times.

It's like thinking about some Thug you don't want to think about. Then sometimes you start doing something normally and after some time you realize you are repeating an action several times a day. And then you realize that if you don't do it, you just feel stressed. For no reason, you know it's stupid, but you know you need to do it! It's like having any other fear which you know is stupid but is really stressful. It's destructive. It's exhausting, and you suffer very much because you know you don't want to do it or think about it. You cannot tell anyone, and they cannot understand anyway. They will try to stop you or just tell you that you are not normal.

I would like society to know what OCD is! I think depression is an ailment people know a little about. But what about OCD? No one knows what it is, so they just think it is people doing weird things: Sto arrivando! Crazy! When I had a very bad episode two years ago, I lost my friends and my boyfriend because they thought I was not normal. I think that maybe Italy is a bit of a particular case perhaps. People have a lot of taboos about illnesses. I guess that if I was maybe in the United States I could say to people that I'm seeing a psychologist without the fear of being abandoned by everybody but my parents.

* * * *

I'm a single 24-year-old white male. I was born in Tennessee where I currently work in a family business.

I think I was in junior high when my OCD began starting to show, but I didn't know what it was. That was my first time going to the counselor for help with regards to excessive worrying. I got better in high school, but everything changed when I graduated.

Starting college made things spiral out of control, and I had to go to counseling again with a different counselor. I was worrying and had a lot of anxiety, but

I didn't know it was OCD. I would worry about everything (checking the stove, fridge, sinks, etc.). I was even afraid of chemicals. I would have to do a ritual if I passed any chemicals that involved spitting. Sometimes I would spit so much because I thought I accidentally swallowed some of the chemicals. Sometimes it would make my throat sore and I couldn't swallow any food or water for a while.

It wasn't until later that I found out that these behaviors were a part of OCD. I found out I had OCD while taking courses for my Psychology degree and seeing another counselor. Currently my OCD consists of checking things over and over again to make sure they are closed or locked (doors, car doors, car windows, etc.). My treatment is good so far with my current counselor. I'm learning techniques to manage my anxiety and reduce my OCD tendencies. I am in a much better place than in the past. I would say my OCD severity level would have been sky high in the past, but now my severity level is much lower. It has been a rough ride, but I take it day by day.

I want people to know that OCD is much more than what you see on TV or in the media. It's a far more complex disorder than people know. It's not just washing your hands, putting things in order, or cleaning constantly. OCD can be constantly worrying or overthinking about things, constantly checking things to make sure they are closed or locked, even obsessing about things that other people would not pay attention to, and so much more. OCD is an exhausting disorder and is different for anyone who has it. It is real, and people should not joke about it.

I have OCD, but that's not who I am. I am a human

just like everyone else. OCD is not easy to deal with, but I fight back. I just wish people would be more open-minded with people who suffer from mental illness. It's a real struggle. Just because you can't see OCD on the surface, doesn't mean someone is not suffering inside. Be kind to everyone, because you don't know what they are going through.

* * * *

I'm a white 23-year-old female. I live in Oregon and I'm an artist. I have Pure-O OCD, which means the compulsions aren't as visible as other forms of OCD are and the thoughts are my biggest struggle. I was diagnosed my junior year of high school. I avoided therapy for a long time, in denial that my medication was enough, but my compulsions and avoidance rituals never went away, I just convinced myself it was fine. I'm in therapy now using the ERP method. It's been difficult so far, maybe because I spent so many years avoiding it, the resistance is stronger now, but I keep at it.

OCD is like your brain is a record player that won't stop skipping over the same part and you can't change the record no matter how much you try. Instead of music the record keeps scratching over your worst nightmares again and again.

I'd like people to stop saying they're "so OCD" when they're really just nit-picky about something. Everyone has things they like a certain way, that's not OCD. I told a classmate I had OCD in high school and she responded by saying "oh, I think everyone is a little OCD about something" and it felt awful to have her invalidate my struggles with OCD like that even though I know she didn't mean any harm.

* * * *

I'm a 23-year-old, non-binary white folk, residing in the Midwest (USA). I am single, and work as a freelance designer. I'm also a graduate student.

My OCD appeared around the age of six and got significantly worse after experiencing recurring violent trauma. I have orderliness and checking OCD. I tried CBT and medication with no avail.

Having OCD is like having an invisible fly floating near your ear constantly buzzing, you can try and swat it away but with no success. It just keeps buzzing. I want people to know that if I could turn off my OCD and live a normal life, I would have already done that.

* * * *

I'm a 22-year-old female. I'm white and I live in the USA where I attend college. I was diagnosed with OCD at age 15 but had symptoms since early childhood. My symptoms would range from counting everything in 4's such as checking to make sure all the doors in my house were locked 4 times, to circling back around a street two or three times to make sure the pot hole my car hit was not a person. Treatment included CBT and medicine which helped tremendously.

I would describe OCD as an itch that you can't scratch, no matter what you do or use to try and scratch it. It's the constant voices in your head telling you that something bad is going to happen to you, your family, or your friends if you don't do something to stop the scratch.

OCD is so much more than just cleanliness and

making sure everything is in order. It's not a trend or a fun quiz to see "how OCD are you". It is real, and it is a daily battle.

* * * *

I am a psychiatric nurse. I'm 33 years old, and I'm a single white female. I'm from Western Pennsylvania. My OCD started when I was 13. I was in a car accident. We were lucky to get out with minor injuries. But, I began to be afraid of riding in cars. I had to be as aware of the road as the driver. I had to pray a specific prayer before I got in the car. I saw a therapist, but it was more like talk therapy.

When I was 14, I began having intrusive thoughts that I would die when I was 15. It was awful. The thoughts were awful, and they wouldn't leave. I told my mom, and she said not to dwell on it. But, that began a nightly ritual of getting reassurance that I was okay. I was reminded that according to the Bible, nobody knows the day or the hour. My mind pushed it even further, and I began having thoughts that I would kill myself. It felt so real. I was even having visions of my dad's guns. I told my therapist about this, but we just did more talk therapy. She wanted me to start meds, but my parents and I refused. This was the 90's, and meds weren't well known about. I was repeating a specific mantra in my head to calm myself. The thoughts finally stopped after several months.

I had Health OCD symptoms after that (fears of cancer or some other deadly disease), over the years. Then, in 2006, the suicide thoughts came back. I had graduated from nursing school, got my job, and moved on my own to the city for the first time. And, my grandparents died. I was diagnosed with OCD during this process. I also hid the knives, because I was afraid I would stab myself in the chest. The images felt very real. I briefly saw a therapist, but I didn't stick with it. I tried Zoloft, but I went on and off of it. When I tried to get back on it the final time, I was grinding my teeth. So, I ditched it. These symptoms lasted until mid-2007. I again just had the cancer fears over the years.

Then, in 2013, I began having thoughts that I needed to make sure everyone followed the rules exactly or I would be fired from my job. I checked everything with my managers. I also worried when parents or my coworkers would be touching my patients' private parts at all. I even worried about the patients touching each other when playing games. I also needed to confess everything. I also had harm and sexual thoughts toward everyone. So, I avoided touching anyone in private areas at all, including my own. I began seeing an OCD specialist weekly, but I was extremely resistant to meds. Now, it was because I knew the side effects! I also was afraid of contaminating others with blood borne diseases. I continued to get worse, and my bosses forced me to get more help. So, I began meds, and I started intensive outpatient therapy. It changed my life.

I learned all about OCD and the hybrid of treatments (CBT with ERP, DBT, etc.) I did hardcore exposures. I had homework between each session. It was so hard, but so worth it. It took two months for everything to click, and then I stayed for another month after that. I'm seeing my regular OCD therapist every two weeks, and I'm still seeing the doctor from the IOP for meds. That combination is what's best for me, and I'm so much better now. I have slid back some since leaving the IOP, but I am able to manage it and stay on top of things. Life is much more enjoyable now.

Everyone gets bizarre and scary thoughts. Most people can let them go. But, due to a chemical imbalance and faulty wiring in our brains, ours stick. We are always in fight or flight mode. These thoughts set off alarm signals in our brains that they must be dealt with. So, we do the compulsions to get rid of the anxiety and stop the thoughts. But, it actually continues the cycle. So, we need to face our fears without doing the compulsions, so we can break the cycle.

My OCD isn't who I am. It is a part of me, but it doesn't define me. I'm so much more than OCD. I'm a nurse who loves my patients. I like to take care of everyone, which includes family, friends, and those I love. My OCD has made me more compassionate and understanding to those with special needs and mental illness. OCD isn't a joke. It's your own personal hell coming from within. But, it can be managed, and you can have a great life.

* * * *

I am a 21-year-old female college student from California. I firmly believe I have had OCD for my entire life, however my breaking point was age 10. That is when my OCD was so severe I feared school and feared teachers. My OCD manifested in the inability to focus. My brain was always spinning so fast I could not focus on daily tasks. My anxiety was so severe at age 16 that I started medication, but I was not actually diagnosed with OCD until the age of 19. I then had much better success with medication and CBT.

OCD feels like you have two brains — a rational brain and an irrational brain. And they're constantly fighting. Not only are they constantly fighting, you never know which is going to win, and it's scary. OCD is a part of me, but it does not define me. I am not my OCD. It's not just being neat, or clean, or 'type A'. It is scary, it's real, but you can overcome it.

* * * *

I am a 20-year-old white, female, college student. I was born in Williamsport, Pennsylvania. I am an English major and am currently single.

I have OCD and one of its "cousins", BDD. My OCD was officially diagnosed senior year of high school, though I'm sure I've always had it. I was convinced I was using stolen money to buy my clothes, coffee, etc. While that symptom has gone largely to the wayside, three years later I am dealing with intrusive thoughts OCD. I keep thinking I have masturbated to or around children. It has waxed and waned but is currently moderate-severe. My BDD was diagnosed a year and a half ago- I became obsessed over some minor acne after a breakup. It is now moderate, though it was severe. While I have long since had therapy, my three-month time in Roger Behavioral Health is what helped both the most.

OCD can be described like how in cartoons, sometimes an angel and a devil sit on opposite sides of the protagonist's shoulder, trying to convince him to choose their way. The OCD is the devil. But the catch is, it looks and sounds exactly like me. Any kid watching the cartoon knows the main character shouldn't listen to the devil, and so do I. But that can be insanely difficult when you can't tell what the devil looks like.

OCD and BDD, especially the former, attack what you value most in life. It is an incredibly unfair illness that can leave intelligent, good people feeling horrible and alone. If talking about it wasn't so taboo, maybe people with OCD wouldn't feel like they are carrying around a big secret all the time.

* * * *

I'm a 23-year-old, white female. I'm an animation student in Philadelphia. I was born in Cleveland; Ohio and I've been with my partner for eight years now.

I've had OCD my whole life, and like others, I had no idea what it was until about four years ago.

OCD feels like everything you've known to be true about your life and yourself is wrong. It feels like your world is crumbling before you and you can only do things to slow the process, but never stop it. I try, but I suffer almost every day. I want people to know that I'm still trying to follow my dreams and be happy.

* * * *

I'm 36 years old. I'm white, non-binary, and was born in Monterey, California. I am a Supported Education Counselor and Tutor, and I'm single.

I have ruminations and scrupulosity OCD triggered by a manic event. The onset was around age 10. It was very severe in my early teens. I had cognitive behavioral therapy in my teens. Starting in my thirties I was medicated with SSRIs and I'm being treated for bipolar disorder. I have very few OCD symptoms on my current medications (lithium, sertraline, and wellbutrin.)

If I were to describe OCD I'd use the analogy of having to use the bathroom really badly... only going to the bathroom will fix it. With OCD, only a certain behavior will relieve the anxiety/stress you experience. As a little kid, that meant turning off the light the right way before I could leave the house or going to confession to confess the most minor of things. I obsessed about being "evil" and analyzed every thought for its morality. It especially affected my reading: I needed to read things "perfectly" so I would read the same sentences over and over. Living with my brain is a kind of torture.

* * * *

I'm 22 years old. I'm a female Caucasian, and I live in America. I work in the research ethics field. I'm unmarried.

My OCD involves A variety of intrusive sexual thoughts and fears. I was in high school at the onset. I'm being treated now for the first time. I had occasional, but persistent symptoms for years. In the last six months it has truly started to distress me, and then I had a nervous breakdown two weeks ago while running a fever. I went to the doctor and immediately started seeing a therapist. The symptoms are currently pretty severe. I have no compulsions that we can determine. However, I'm responding well to treatment and medication.

OCD for me is less about the obsession, and more about the intense fear and psychological distress. Our brain often generates random, senseless thoughts that are objectively weird or disturbing. Normally, a healthy person can brush these off. A person with OCD experiences intense emotion in regard to the thought, which is then the beginning of an obsession. These thoughts don't have any reflection on what we would do. We have the strong reactions because whatever it is, it is completely contrary to our core values. It could be literally anything, and that changes nothing about our value as people.

* * * *

I'm a 23-year-old, female. I'm British and live in Manchester, England. I work full time and I'm single. I've had OCD since the age of seven. I have intrusive thoughts that are sexual and violent. My rituals include licking taps, tapping, and even self-induced vomiting. If I had to describe OCD to someone who knows nothing about it, I would tell them it is a monster that takes over your life. It is a mental illness - it's not about cleaning.

* * * *

I'm a 27-year-old, Caucasian, female from Atlanta, Georgia. I'm also a stay at home mom to two young boys.

The first onset of symptoms that I can recall started around my freshman year of high school. The earliest memory of OCD I have was going through the lunch line and touching multiple milks, picking some up and switching them for others to get the "right" milk so that a loved one wouldn't die while I was at school that day. Later in life, I learned the name for what I had been suffering from.

I don't have any particular type of OCD, as my

themes change frequently. I've struggled from harm OCD, tying my hands together in my sleep to make sure I didn't harm anyone. Driving up and down roads, over and over, scanning the sides for pedestrians that I may have hit. I have also had a theme of contamination, in specifically, HIV. I ended up spending hundreds and hundreds of dollars being repeatedly tested and shedding so many tears, losing so many nights of sleep just sure that I was HIV positive. Even though test after tests revealed that I was in fact, HIV negative. Those are just a few examples. Over the years, I've seen multiple therapists and a psychiatrist. I've taken multiple medicines and tried CBT and medication to feel better. I have even shamefully, at times, self-medicated with alcohol to escape my symptoms.

OCD is A living hell. It's self-doubt. It's reassurance seeking. It's constantly worrying if your thoughts are a product of your disorder or a sure sign that you are a horrible person. I want people to know that it isn't just about being organized, neat, cleanly or particular. It's debilitating.

* * * *

I'm a 35-year-old white male. I live in Madison, Wisconsin. I'm married with one child.

I'm currently in outpatient OCD treatment at Rodgers Memorial Hospital in Madison, Wisconsin. We're playing around with the idea that I have TOCD. I have phrases I have to say when I have flashes of embarrassing or uncomfortable thoughts as well as other compulsions.

I have irrational thoughts that form compulsions to "ease" the anxiety. It's not easily controlled. It's painful to control. My thoughts come out of the blue and cause anxiety.

* * * *

I'm a 21-year-old female who has been on leave from college for a few semesters because of mental health challenges. I was diagnosed the summer after third grade. It began with a fear of monsters. I had a long checking ritual before going to bed and spent frequent nights in my parents' room. My OCD turned into a fear of burglars after a horrific murder in my town. I grew out of the severity of these symptoms, though some checking and tapping and fear of certain numbers and not right feelings have lingered.

When I was 16, I developed a fear of eating fats, leading to food restriction and hospitalization, and then this led to the development of an eating disorder. Since that time, I have gone back and forth from residential to partial programs and to outpatient treatment for a combination of the eating disorder and OCD, keeping me from missing three months of high school my senior year and on leave from college. Eating fats, food in general (which is part OCD, part ED), and fluids (which is part OCD, part depression) causes dissociative episodes or panic attacks.

OCD is a psychological monster that puts thoughts into your brain that you don't realize aren't you and aren't rational until you are caught in its grips. After you do realize the irrationality it is hardly an easier task to challenge the thoughts and not act on behaviors. And OCD doesn't act on its own: it leads to feelings of isolation leading to depression and a lack of hope--especially after that voice in your head tells you that you should have gotten better by now.

OCD isn't something that you find complete recovery from. There is still that voice, there are still the lingering behaviors. Living and functioning with OCD requires supportive people and people willing to try to understand to help you.

40's and 50's

I'm a 41-year-old white male. I'm married, and I sell real estate. The onset of my OCD really started in my mid to late 20's. A panic attack unexpectedly brought it on and it evolved into more panic and that led to OCD. I have irrational unwanted urges or thoughts that encumbers me every day. It can feel like the most crippling disease at times and it is a daily battle.

OCD is something that is challenging every day and much more common than people think. I want people to understand that it affects people from all walks of life. You can't tell someone has it and like other mental diseases, it often goes untreated for years.

* * * *

I am a 58-year-old white female born and raised in northern California. I have lived in the beautiful state of Idaho for the past 25 years. I've been married to my wonderful husband for 35 years, and we have two adult boys, a 5-year-old grandson, and another grandson on the way. I used to work as an administrative assistant while living in California, but I was able to be a full-time mom when we moved to Idaho. I was a substitute teacher in our local elementary school and also volunteered regularly in the classroom.

I was always a very anxious child and a constant worrier. My mother had severe OCD (contamination and washing) and her bizarre rituals ruled our family life. We were never ever allowed to have any friends or family (outside of my mom, dad, and three brothers) come inside our home, with the exception of my grandparents on very few occasions. My mom's sister and her family lived very close to us, but they were never allowed into our home. My aunt would be knocking at the door and my mom would talk to her through the kitchen window and always come up with some excuse why she couldn't "visit" right then. We were, however, able to go over to other people's homes as a family; but, we could never reciprocate in our own home.

I was around 13 when I first realized something was terribly wrong with me. I adored my little brother, who was 12 years younger than me, and one day it just suddenly occurred to me how easy it would be to kill him. The thought both horrified and terrified me. My little brother was so innocent and vulnerable, and I loved him so much. How or why would I have this heinous thought come into my mind. That was the beginning of my living nightmare. I was afraid to be alone with him, which was hard because I always had to babysit him. I tried to keep my mind and my life constantly busy and occupied in order to get relief from the thoughts. Then when I started babysitting other children outside our home, I started to wonder what would stop me from sexually abusing children. Again, I was horrified and terrified at the content of these thoughts. I also began obsessively checking things, like locked doors or making sure I had turned off the stove, and so forth.

When I married, the thoughts centered on "what if I wake up in the middle of the night and kill my husband?" Then when I had my own children, I was plagued with "what if I kill my own children?" When I was around 30, I was consumed by uncontrollable anxiety and these thoughts on the inside, but I appeared perfectly normal on the outside, working full-time and caring for my family. Finally, it got to be too much, and I had a breakdown. I had to tell my husband everything I was going through and finally looked for help. That is another story, because back in the mid-to-late 1980s, knowledge about OCD was in its infancy. I finally found a doctor at Stanford in Palo Alto, California, who was working with the early trials of fluoxetine (Prozac). Unfortunately, I did not qualify for the trials, as I had anxiety disorder combined with OCD, but I was still able to be given Prozac, and it changed my life.

My dosage has fluctuated over the years. Right now, I am on 20 mg once a day, but I've been taking it at some amount non-stop for almost 30 years. The thoughts still haunt me, but it feels like I'm able to shut the door on them. They are still there, in my mind, but they don't plague me non-stop any more. I can choose to not spend time ruminating on them. I constantly live in fear that the Prozac effect will one day wear off. I fear I will be sucked back into OCD's hell while being with my grandson. However, then I forget about it all and just try to live my life to the fullest.

OCD is this internal demon from hell. It's not like hearing voices, but rather it is my own thoughts questioning over and over and over. It makes absolutely no difference how irrational the thoughts are. I know they are irrational. I know I'm not a killer or a child molester. I know I did lock the door and turn the stove off. But whatever process of the mind that is supposed to recognize and ensure that knowledge and allow my mind to move on and past these thoughts does not work right. My mind feels stuck in a loop, like an endless merry-go-round in hell. I want to jump off...not to my death, but to freedom. However, I simply cannot do that on my own. Somehow the Prozac gets me off the hellish merry-go-round, but I wish I could get rid of it for good one day. It's terribly difficult to explain or describe it to anyone, especially the pure obsessions. Even my mom, whose compulsions were many and had a strong hold over her, could not understand what I was talking about when I tried to explain the obsessions that constantly swirled about my mind. For the longest time, I think she feared that I was mentally ill, while never understanding that she was equally so. Neither of us could fully comprehend the manifestations of the other's OCD.

I've been to hell and back with OCD. I would not wish that journey on my worst enemy. OCD is like cancer of the mind. It often cannot be seen or touched or made evident in any way, but it is constantly eating away at who I am, who I want to be. I am not my OCD. I do not embrace having OCD. Don't tell me that my struggle has made me who I am today. I get very angry when people say about their quirky "habits" – "Oh, I'm soooo OCD." People need to understand that this is as insensitive as stating, "Oh, look my hair is getting so thin. I feel like a cancer patient." Think before you speak.

* * * *

I'm a 40-year-old white female. I was born in Illinois. I work in retail and I'm single. My OCD started when I was a child. I can't remember the exact age. My OCD centers around checking, contamination, and intrusive thoughts. It's been severe enough to keep me inside the house when I don't want to stay in the house. I've had 20 years of therapy, and medication treatment.

OCD feels as though my brain has taken over my body and forces it to do things it does not want to do. It is exhausting. It really irritates me when people lightly use the term "OCD" when they really don't have or know anything about OCD.

* * * *

I'm a 46-year-old white female. I'm married and live in England.

I have had OCD episodes several times over the years with periods of being fine in-between. The episodes were triggered by extreme stress and stopping medication. They lasted months at a time and were usually stopped by medication. When I would stop medication, the cycle would begin again.

OCD is like your brain is never quiet. It feels like your brain is against you and does and thinks anything it can to make you feel like a bad person. You become your own worst enemy. OCD can be overcome. There is no reason to be ashamed. People who struggle with OCD deserve help and support. Remember, you are a good person and OCD is only a part of you and not all of who you are.

* * * *

I am a 52-year-old single mom born in the Bronx, New York. I have been working as an Administrative Assistant to the Director of Rehab at a Long-Term Care Facility. I would say my OCD symptoms started to appear around the age of four years old, but became more disabling in my teens, and skyrocketed during late my 20's. What started out as a small symptom of having to count 100 kisses on my mom's cheek when saying goodbye has developed to the present where I am battling tics and twitches that I actually have to count. In between all of these behaviors were the common symptoms of checking lights and doors up to 16 times and washing my hands to raw. I have been in treatment at same healthcare clinic since 1992.

My OCD is really crippling at times. My mind is constantly hitting rewind over and over and over. It's exhausting and humiliating. As is the case nowadays with the saying, "I am sooo OCD." People with true, professionally diagnosed OCD choose not to broadcast this exhausting and humiliating disease.

* * * *

I am a 51-year-old woman born in Rhode Island, currently living in Philadelphia. I am unmarried, and I work part-time training dogs. I've never known life without OCD. My parents used to tell me about how neatly I'd put my toys away after playing with them in a play pen. My OCD initially had everything to do with perfectionism and always being "good". As I got older it took on more common aspects such as cleanliness, washing, contamination, tapping, and having things feel "just right". When I was in my early 20's I was hospitalized for anorexia. It had a lot of OCD components to it but back then it was the early '90s, and OCD was not commonly diagnosed. I was treated for depression and anxiety with medications and ECT treatments. I was hospitalized many, many times with the professionals never catching the diagnosis of OCD.

In 2000 I found a new doctor and I told him, "I think I have OCD" and we proceeded from there. In 2001 I went to the OCD Institute in Belmont, Massachusetts and I really learned about ERP and how to really deal with my obsessions and compulsions. When I left I started working and I felt so much better. I continued seeing a therapist and a psychiatrist until 2005 when I decided I'd move far away from my triggers and start all over. I got a puppy and the OCD sprang back into my life. I started having obsessions about the dog: I wasn't a good pet owner, I would hurt the dog, I was neglectful, my dog was contaminated, and so on. In November, I returned to the OCD Institute and started over again, this time working on harm obsessions.

When I returned to my home I again returned to work and did "ok", but it was a solitary life and I wanted to find others to talk to, so in 2007, I attended my first International OCD Foundation (IOCDF) Conference in Houston. I met Dr. Grayson and went "Virtual Camping". I was elated by my new-found ability to do "gross" things. I started working with Dr. Grayson by phone after that Conference and eventually he coaxed me into moving to Philadelphia to work with him more intensely. In 2009 I sold my house and moved to Philly where I've been making ongoing progress since. I'll always have OCD but now it is mainly background noise. I can do most of the things that people without OCD can do. I often offer support to other sufferers and used to help out in a support group. Every day is a new adventure and OCD no longer controls my life.

If I had to describe OCD to someone who knew nothing about it I would tell them to imagine their worst fears and tell them those fears will continue to echo in their heads continuously unless they give into some silly actions. And then repeat, over and over, every day without stopping.

I want people to know that OCD isn't fun. It isn't "cool". It's not about cleaning or being organized. It's about living with crippling anxiety every day and falling asleep each night exhausted by performing rituals and being tied up with anxiety. It's never useful or "quirky". It's a horrible disorder but there is plenty of help and hope.

* * * *

I live in London, England with my partner. I'm a 44-year-old black taxi driver. I was diagnosed with OCD at 28-years-old. I have Pure-O intrusive thoughts. It started when I was 21 years old. I got treatment that included CBT, seroxat, sertraline, and Prozac. My thought spectrum went from homosexual to pedophilic to rage and harm OCD then killing OCD.

The stereotype of OCD is washing hands, checking, contamination, but not a lot is mentioned around harm or homosexual or pedophile OCD. I would say to them that OCD is a horrific debilitating disorder, a scary one that makes you think you're actually an evil person.

I want people to know that there is hope, and that the

thoughts that enter your mind don't make you the person that you think you are. The thoughts go against the grain and they attack you and make you feel like a very bad person.

* * * *

I'm a 49-year-old female of European and Native American descent. I was born in the United States. I'm an author and I'm married. I have Pure- O obsessive thoughts on and off. I believe there is a genetic link now that we know about the study of cherry blossoms scent associated with mice behavior, it is not learned transference of a genuine perceived threat through genes. I think it happens with humans as it seems related to fears of family members dying, fear of the future, etc.

For me, OCD is hell created by thoughts. Unfortunately, there is a stigma associated with mental illness. People are lonely, and it's made worse because they feel they have to keep it a secret for fear of losing their job or their social contacts.

* * * *

I'm a 47-year-old Caucasian female. I'm from Wilmington, Delaware. I'm married and have a degree in painting and drawing. I run my own cat-sitting business.

I can remember when my OCD started. It was one evening when I was around age seven. I put my doll down in her crib and suddenly I felt the need to repeat, repeat, repeat the process or I would get sick, throw up, or die. The severity has changed over the years from handwashing, checking, repeat tasks, and counting. My

OCD is most severe when people are sick around me.

OCD is really like being haunted every minute of every day by irrational unwanted obsessive thoughts that force me to do repetitive behaviors to rid my mind of an overwhelming fear of getting sick or dying.

As a child I thought of my OCD as my religion. It was a way for me to control my world so that I felt safe. It's very irrational, but even knowing this does not alleviate the need to stop doing rituals. It's overwhelming and senseless but I can't stop. OCD is both my best friend and my worst enemy. I wouldn't want any child of mine to grow up feeling as crappy as I did, thus I never wanted to have children. Most of my life I have felt that I would like to disappear—to go to bed and not wake up would be a blessing; the end of my tortured mind. I have learned to control it over the years, but it is always hovering next to me, waiting to take over.

* * * *

I'm 52 years old. I am married, and I have two children. I run a bar and I do sales work.

My OCD started at the age of seven or eight. I just remember feeling mortal fears. I have been through a lot. My fears run the whole gamut from fear of poisons, causing someone to be ill, harming my family. It has never gone away. It is such a crushing horrible disease. It will steal your life if you let it. I am a good person and despite my illness I carry on. I employ a lot of people and I love my family and they all understand me.

* * * *

I am a 59-year-old female, Caucasian. I was born in northern Maine and live in a very rural area. I have a degree in nursing. I am married with three adult children and eight grandchildren. I used to be a foreign missionary but the OCD, and eventually the co-morbid major depression, caused me to change my profession, my ministry and my physical location. If I had asked for help and known that there was hope, I could have stayed on in a ministry that I worked at so hard to get to where I was. My original intent was to do that for my entire career. We moved back to the US because I believed that there would be more resources available, I could get help in English, and it would be less stressful to be in my own culture.

I thought my OCD happened suddenly, when the intrusive thoughts began, as I did not consider my other, milder symptoms to be abnormal. I now understand that it began at eight years old but was limited to a couple of obsessions that didn't consume my life. It started to get worse when we were training to live in a third-world country. Contamination and checking were my main issues but, again, these did not consume me, just caused anxiety in the moment. Then, after my third child had been born and we were living overseas, the intrusive thoughts began seemingly out of nowhere. I was walking my baby to sleep when they started. Then checking doors and locks soon became a serious and time-consuming issue. It involved counting and checking and got worse over time. Soon it was joined by contamination issues.

It was the intrusive thoughts, blasphemous and sexual in nature, which were horrific to me, and that really sent me on a downward spiral. I am a committed

Christian. I didn't know what was happening and was too scared to ask for help. I went on suffering for four years, spiraling downward and adding new obsessions and compulsions on a regular basis. It snowballed until it affected every area of my life. It was that severe. It consumed my life and caused shame, severe anxiety and major depression. I did not want to ask for help as I wanted to appear strong and I expected others to not understand and to be judgmental.

I became suicidal. I got help finally because my husband insisted once he found out. I went to a counselor who insisted that I see a psychiatrist and get on medication before I started counseling. That was 25 years ago. My first medication was Anafranil, effective but with major side effects. I have always needed the highest doses of the medicines to be effective against the OCD, and when decreasing doses to switch medicines, the intrusive thoughts would start again. After two years, I went to a new psychiatrist who changed the medicine to Prozac. I also got back into counseling for the depression.

Since we moved a lot, after another four years, I had a different psychiatrist and was put on Luvox, Wellbutrin SR and Buspar. That combo worked well but I still had side effects that I did not want, and it decreased my quality of life. I was on the maximum dose of Luvox and was able to work as a Labor and Delivery nurse, a real challenge for someone with contamination issues. I was on Luvox for five years until I got off it.

So, I was on anti-OCD meds for 11 years in total. There was and is no one in my area that is trained in ERP therapy, so I read about it and slowly worked on it by myself. I now consider myself free of the worst of OCD. I have had exacerbations of the OCD, in times of additional stress. The checking and contamination issues are the main ones that pop up. When obsessions start, and I feel the need to do compulsions, I say to myself, "I'm not going back".

In my profession, I see individual clients and do counseling on chronic medical disease management, but I see real people who are more than just people with a chronic medical disease. I am able to offer help and hope. I give them a safe place to talk. I am better able to help others because I have struggled with it myself.

OCD has taught me how to be humble, to admit that I have problems and to ask for help. It has taught me that mental illness is no respecter of persons. It is distressing, disabling, all-consuming, and makes you feel a prisoner of anxiety. It is demoralizing and devastating. I thought the intrusive thoughts meant that I was a bad person and weak since I could not overcome them. It is not a person's fault. There is help but it will take hard work, courage and persistence to make progress. I have a greater empathy and understanding of others who deal with all kinds of mental illness. I have had to do the hard work and to be patient for results. I want others to be willing to ask for help and to know that there is hope with treatment. OCD is a serious disorder that changes people's lives.

* * * *

I'm a 46-year-old white female. I was born in Albany, New York. I work as a Speech Pathologist in public schools. I am divorced and have no children.

I have concerns with contamination, specifically pesticides. I have had OCD since I was about seven, but this big trigger about specific pesticides happened about 30 years ago, in my teens. I have been in outpatient and inpatient treatment for about 20 years. It is very difficult for me to do ERP as I feel so strongly that someone will die if I do not check for pesticides everywhere. I work but have limited social interaction and my relationships are limited to my parents and my sister.

OCD is a debilitating disease. I understand my compulsions, rituals, and triggers sound bizarre, but I strongly feel that someone in my family will die if I do not check or clean things from potential pesticides. My OCD is challenging because there are pesticides in the world, and they can kill people if ingested. However, my trigger is specific from 30 years ago and I have to realize that the potential for this pesticide to still be around or toxic is quite small.

I am not crazy or weird, although I may do strange things, or rituals. I don't worry about hurting myself; I just worry about hurting my loved ones. I would rather have a physical disability or illness, which is visible, acceptable and tolerated. OCD is not. I pray every day that I can die.

* * * *

I'm a 42-year-old Caucasian female. I was born in Beaumont, Texas. I'm married and work as a Nuclear Medicine Technologist.

My OCD centers around checking and contamination. The checking has been with me for as long and I can remember. The contamination is more recent within the last five years. I also have OCD spectrum issues as well, which includes Trichotillomania. The Trich started around age 12. I have never been formally diagnosed, however, I have generalized anxiety and panic as well with some depression. In the past I took SSRIs for my anxiety for several years. I have also been to therapy in the past and am currently going again.

OCD feels like you are trapped in your mind at times, and even though you know it is irrational, the checking and hand washing that you feel you have to do, you just can't stop because doing those things makes you feel less anxious.

Even though I have the OCD and anxiety, I have managed to become a successful individual with a husband and family. I graduated from college and though I struggle, I lean on my faith, family and therapy to get me through it. You can learn to manage symptoms. I have times that are worse than others and times where it is not so bad. It will always be a part of me, but I am doing what I can to not let it get the best of me.

* * * *

I am 51-year-old white man born in Odessa, Texas. I am a Small Business Advisor and adjunct faculty in business at The University of Houston- Downtown. I am recently widowed.

I noticed my OCD beginning in seventh grade. It was a stressful school year for me and I was bullied. I started having strange thoughts. I felt I had to retrace my path during the day and if I didn't I'd end up in an alternative universe or something. I say or something because really the fear is nebulous and not very clear. I ended up having to go through doorways a certain number of times in order to not be contaminated but I didn't know what from. I did a lot of counting as well.

As I did these things my OCD gradually expanded to almost everything I did. I had to do it a certain number of times. Many times, I would try to think of good things when I did something, like pick up a glass so that I wasn't contaminated by "bad" things. This repeating and magical thinking became a huge part of my life. I literally spent hours a day doing this, eventually it was all day and soon after I could not dress myself, bathe myself, or even eat without the help of my parents and brother because it was too overwhelming. Once I got treatment I gained 95% recovery.

OCD is nonsensical thoughts that you can't dismiss because there is some fear, some impending doom, that if you don't act to neutralize it bad things will happen. The crazy thing is you know it is nonsense and there is nothing to worry about, but your brain floods you with this terror so strong you can't ignore it. It makes you feel completely crazy.

In fact, I hid my OCD from my parents and friends for years because I felt crazy and felt stigma of being mentally ill. I thought if people knew it would bring shame to me and my family. I felt it would end any career aspirations I had. I also felt it affected my moral character. I want anyone with any mental illness to know it is not a moral failing. You are not inferior. It is just a disease like asthma that you need treatment for. Seek help.

* * * *

I'm a 41-year-old Caucasian female. I was born in Fountain Valley California. I'm a Customer Service Supervisor, and I'm divorced.

I have Responsibility OCD which started showing severe signs at 24 years of age. I tried many treatments, and nothing helped until I attended the UCLA outpatient treatment program.

OCD is intrusive thoughts that torture you every day. It is hard to know what is reality or an intrusive thought because the thoughts feel so real. It is a fight within oneself. OCD is a terrorist in your head constantly trying to terrorize you. In order to feel better about the terrorism going on in your head, you use compulsions to alleviate some of that terror going on in your head. You literally feel if you don't perform compulsions that you could be responsible for catastrophic events.

OCD is thoughts in your head and you cannot tell if they are real or not. The thoughts are so powerful they make you think they are real. OCD is so much more than the stereotype of being organized and clean. OCD is pure brain terror that feels so real it literally can wear someone down, so they feel hopeless and out of control of their own self.

* * * *

I'm a 43-year-old white male. I was born in Livingston, New Jersey. I'm a teacher, and I'm single. I don't want to share anything about my OCD. I do want people to know that having OCD is paralyzing and takes quite a toll on your health. I'm a hard-working person that allowed the OCD to bite back at me and I'm trying to white-knuckle it right now, but I have been seeking help for about two months.

* * * *

I am a 48-year-old wife and mother of four. I was born and raised and reside in Pennsylvania. I suppose I have always had signs of OCD. I recall being young and having to recite a litany I made up to keep bad thoughts out of my mind. I also recall being in college and making tally marks as I recited my litany during class. I held my OCD at bay until I hit age 40. Then suddenly...I had the most severe panic attack I ever imagined. My OCD manifested itself in the form of Health Anxiety, specifically fear of cancer. I finally sought treatment from my primary care physician, who was so understanding and compassionate! I also had the most compassionate nurse who made me feel safe.

Ugh! I would tell the person who knew nothing about OCD that it is like a sneaky serpent. It slithers around your mind, waiting until it finds the smallest crack. Then it slides in and fills your mind with lies and fears and worries. It is constant, and it is ruthless. I want people to know that OCD isn't a trait of a neat person. It doesn't mean you like to have your glasses lined up. OCD is a disease; one I wouldn't wish upon my worst enemy. And... I have OCD. I am not OCD. Thank you for doing this. God bless!

60's and 70's

I'm 70-years-old. I'm a white female born in Merrill, Wisconsin. I'm divorced. I was a systems analyst but have since retired.

I have contamination OCD. I was 21 at onset. It came on during a dating trauma. I had ECT, SSRIs, meditation, EMDR, hypnosis, and spent nine months in the hospital from 1975-1976. I have very severe handwashing and cleaning OCD.

I think about my OCD as a malfunction of the brain. A fear, sometimes irrational fear, gets trapped in the brain, and that brings severe anxiety, and rituals lessen anxiety no matter how irrational.

There is no cure for OCD. It can be inherited, or it can come from environmental influences. Treatments can help lessen the severity, and symptoms can go up and down in severity, but never give up in pursuing recovery.

* * * *

I'm 73 years old. I'm a white male, from Paul, Idaho. I'm married and work in sales.

My OCD involves checking, and ruminating. I have had it since age 17. I have taken medication and gotten professional help. Even though I would characterize my OCD as mostly mild, it is still very troublesome. OCD is a disorder that destroys a person's life a day at a time. I have worked hard to learn what I can to manage my OCD. I am self-taught and for some people that works best.

* * * *

I'm a 68-year-old white male. I'm married and live in New York. I'm a retired social worker. My OCD started at about age 13. It involves contamination, and intrusive thoughts. I saw several therapists, and finally found one who knew about cognitive behavioral, ERP. At times my OCD has been very severe. It is something you feel you have little control over. I want people to have hope and know that you can get better.

* * * *

I'm a 70-year-old male. I'm white and I live in England. I'm a retired marine.

My OCD started when I was around the age of six. I felt that terrible things would happen if I didn't carry out rituals. I was treated with CBT, ECT, and medication.

OCD dominates my life still. It makes me feel like I can't even describe what I'm feeling to you. If you asked me what it is like to have OCD I am not sure if I would be allowed to tell you.

* * * *

I'm a 70-year-old white male. I was born in Tennessee. I'm single, and a retired software developer.

I've had various symptoms of OCD throughout my life. The primary ones are checking and contamination. I was diagnosed at age 40 but have experienced non-disabling symptoms since childhood. I was treated after diagnosis, including individual and group therapy. I was briefly hospitalized twice and was on short-term disability at work on one of those occasions.

OCD is like having your brain get stuck on some idea or thought that absorbs all, or most of your attention. Usually it is associated with significant fear which most people would not understand. It can be very disabling, but it is an illness, not a person's personality. Don't mix it up with minor traits like being orderly or focusing on having a clean house. Avoid "he/she is so OCD." No such thing— you have a serious disorder, OCD, or you don't. Read and learn about it.

* * * *

I'm a 71-year-old Caucasian male. I worked in social work in Michigan. I was divorced and now am remarried. I've got fears of hurting others or myself through mental ramification. I also have religious guilt and fears associated with that form of OCD. I have had many different symptoms of many forms of OCD over the years.

I remember the first onset of my anxiety in mid-grade school. I actually found out about OCD from Ann landers in 1990. I have moderate severity and have been treated at the University of Michigan by Joseph Himle, Ph.D.

For people who don't know what having OCD is like I would describe it as repetitive, anxiety provoking, seeking reassurance behavior. I have struggled a long time with anxiety and coping but knowing the diagnosis and the methods of coping helped me considerably... Thank you for doing this!

Chapter Eight: The Importance of Advocacy

Ethan Smith

I was once told "the best thing you can do for OCD is help others." At the time, I thought the psychiatrist who told me that was insensitive and rude. I struggled with debilitating OCD. I was currently living in a residential facility. I could barely function let alone, help others. Why wasn't he focusing on me? On my needs? What I wanted? This time was supposed to be about Me! Me! Me!

Advocacy's power is undeniable. It's both an altruistic and selfish act. I love helping others. I love how I feel when I help others. Almost eight years after receiving life-changing treatment after 31 years of misery and suffering at the proverbial hands of OCD, I've discovered one thing to be consistently true: the best thing you can do for OCD is in fact, help others.

Advocacy takes many forms and can be expressed in a variety of ways. I chose to speak openly, publically, and nationally in an effort to make sure no one suffers as I had. I chose to join other amazing advocates in an effort to educate about this more often than not, misunderstood mental illness. In my opinion, however, the most powerful effect that being of service can have is shattering the stigma surrounding mental illness.

Speaking out gives others permission not to hide. It sends a message that having OCD is nothing to be ashamed of or embarrassed about. It's a disease, not a decision. It's no different than diabetes or cancer. Do we judge individuals who suffer from those? Just because it can't be seen on an x-ray, doesn't mean it isn't there.

No one should have to hide in silence. Suffer alone. Not anymore. The most effective way to prevent those things from happening is to advocate large and advocate loud. Ryan is such an amazing example of how one person can make a difference in a way that's important and meaningful. He's a tenacious high school student who decided to advocate and created an avenue to do so... This book.

Stories are a necessary and integral part of advocacy. They're how we relate to each other. They're how we learn we're not alone. They're constant reminders of where we came from and where we don't want to go back to. That's the power of advocacy. In one conversation with one individual YOU can change a person's entire outlook. Give them hope where there was none. Give them strength where there was none. Inspire them to take action. Simultaneously, reminding yourself of all the reasons to continue making the right choices, toward your values, away from OCD. You choose life.

Consistent practice of advocacy, without a doubt, is the best weapon I have against OCD. The thoughts are still there, sometimes whispers, sometimes screams. But I know I can't turn back, because every person I talk to inevitably holds me accountable. That one person impacted my life for the better. And the most amazing part? That person also advocated. Just by confiding in me, sharing their story. Telling their truth. They advocated not only for themselves, but for me.

We are all in this together. Only together can we make a change, start a movement, initiate a revolution. So, no one, ever again, questions the validity of Obsessive Compulsive Disorder. That OCD becomes synonymous with any other debilitating disease and is treated in kind. Then, we'll all live in a world where we don't have to fight stigma, shame, guilt, and embarrassment. We can just focus on what matters. Getting better.

Chapter Nine: The International OCD Foundation

About the International OCD Foundation

The mission of the International OCD Foundation (IOCDF) is to help individuals with obsessive compulsive disorder (OCD) and related disorders live full and productive lives. The IOCDF aims to increase access to effective treatment, end the stigma associated with mental health issues, and foster a community for those affected by OCD and the professionals who treat them.

The International OCD Foundation (IOCDF) is the foremost resource about OCD and related disorders. Thanks to the patronage of members and donors, the IOCDF is able to provide support, education, and resources for those affected by OCD and related disorders, as well as for the professionals who treat them. Based in Boston, the IOCDF has affiliates in 24 states and territories, as well as 11 Global Partners. Since their founding in 1986, the IOCDF has granted millions of dollars for OCD research, trained thousands of professionals to effectively treat OCD, and helped to improve the lives of millions affected by OCD and related disorders.

Examples of IOCDF Programs and Resources Include:

Education & Advocacy

Annual OCD Conference. The Annual OCD Conference brings together the most experienced mental health professionals and OCD researchers alongside individuals with OCD and their families. The Conference provides access to the latest information about OCD and related disorders in a supportive and engaging environment.

1 Million Steps 4 OCD Walk. The 1 Million Steps 4 OCD Walk is an annual grassroots awareness-building and fundraising event that supports the work of the IOCDF, while also increasing awareness about OCD and related disorders.

OCD Awareness Week. OCD Awareness Week is an international effort that takes place annually during the second week in October. OCD Awareness Week helps raise awareness and understanding about OCD and related disorders, with the goal of reducing stigma and advocating for timely access to appropriate and effective treatment.

Resources & Support

Resource Directory. The IOCDF maintains a comprehensive and easy-to-use Resource Directory that includes over 1,200 treatment providers specializing in OCD and/or related disorders, 400 support groups, 70 intensive treatment and specialist outpatient clinics, and their local affiliates and global partners. The Resource Directory can be accessed through the IOCDF homepage (www.iocdf.org).

OCD in Kids, Help for Hoarding, and Help for Body Dysmorphic Disorder Websites. The IOCDF has collaborated with experts to provide additional specialized websites that house vital information, research, and resources for **Hoarding Disorder** (www.helpforhoarding.org), **OCD in Kids** (www.ocdinkids.org), and **Body Dysmorphic Disorder** (www.helpforBDD.org).

IOCDF Affiliates. The IOCDF regional affiliates carry out the mission of the national organization at a local community level. The IOCDF has affiliates in 24 states and territories in the U.S., and they are adding more every year.

Research & Training

Research Grants. The IOCDF is committed to finding and promoting the most effective treatment methods for OCD and related disorders. Since 1994, over $3,000,000 in IOCDF Research Grants have been awarded for research into the causes of, and treatments for, OCD and related disorders.

Scientific and Clinical Advisory Board (SCB). The International OCD Foundation's SCB is comprised of the foremost clinicians and researchers in the U.S. who treat and research OCD and related disorders.

IOCDF Training Institute. The IOCDF Training Institute offers a comprehensive curriculum to train mental health professionals in effective treatments for OCD, which are not typically taught during graduate and medical school training.

Upcoming Resources

The IOCDF continues to expand their resources to meet the needs of the community. They are in the process of launching a **Transition Packet Program**, which will provide information, education, and resources for individuals transitioning out of OCD residential programs, as well as an **Anxiety in the Classroom Program**, which will create an online OCD resource center for school personnel, students, and their families.

Get Involved with The IOCDF

There are many ways that a person can get involved with the IOCDF. Some examples include:

- Become an IOCDF member
- Become an OCDvocate
- Attend an event
- Share your story
- Sign up to receive IOCDF emails

To learn more about ways to get involved, please visit www.iocdf.org/get-involved.

Support the Work of The IOCDF

The IOCDF receives no funding from the city or state. Their work is 100% privately funded thanks to the generosity of members and donors. By becoming an IOCDF member or making a donation, individuals can support the work of IOCDF to increase awareness, reduce stigma, and improve the lives of all those affected by OCD and related disorders.

By purchasing this book, you are supporting the IOCDF because all proceeds from book sales will be donated to the International OCD Foundation. To learn more about these and other IOCDF programs please visit www.iocdf.org.

Acknowledgements

To each of you who courageously shared your story. This book would not have been possible without your desire to make a difference.

To the dedicated professionals who contributed to this book. Thank you for your time and expertise.

To Maureen Brennan, it began with you. Thank you for helping me find the courage to take those first steps. I will be forever grateful.

To Kevin Ashworth, you saw what I couldn't. Thank you for showing me that I could face my fears.

To Ashley Wray, thank you for your caring low-key approach that helped me when I was anxious.

To Dr. Craigan Usher, thank you for always being available and willing to help me whenever I needed it.

To Drew White, you are more than my climbing coach. You are a friend and mentor and have taught me so much about life. Thank you for making a safe welcoming place for me.

To Jeff Szymanski, thank you for all you do through the IOCDF.

To Meghan Buco, thank you for responding to that first email. You were always there to answer every question.

To Ethan Smith, thank you for helping me build an advocacy platform and supporting me at every challenging step along the way.

To Shai Friedland, and my friends at South African Depression and Anxiety Group, thank you for being a wealth of knowledge and taking the time to talk with me.

To the educators who took the time to understand me especially Merrill Hendin, Sam Blumberg, Sheila Kendall, Kelly Milford, Morgan McFadden, Ellen Whatmore, Josh Winnicki, Blair Haddon, Jacob Hockett, JoAnna Coleman, Joe Minato, Mike Duchow-Pressley, Chris Bartlo, and Norman Stremming.

To my dedicated publisher, Barbara Terry, and Waldorf Publishing, thank you for believing in this book.

To my editors, Carol McCrow and Colleen Baxter, thank you for your careful and considerate review.

To all the OCD advocates who encouraged me and who continue to work tirelessly to erase stigma including: Liz McIngvale, Alison Dotson, Morgan Rondinelli, and Janet Singer.

To my grandparents, Honey and Poppee, thank you for always being there no matter what.

To my parents, your constant love and support keeps me going, and to my brother Matthew, you never gave up.

About the Contributors

Dr. Jenny C. Yip, Psy.D., ABPP, is a clinical psychologist, author, speaker, and a nationally recognized OCD and anxiety expert. She developed the Family Systems Based Strategic CBT and has treated severe OCD and anxiety disorders for almost two decades. She's been featured in various media venues and founded the Renewed Freedom Center – Los Angeles in 2008. She's Board Certified in Behavioral & Cognitive Psychology, is Clinical Assistant Professor of Psychiatry at USC Keck School of Medicine, and is the author of "Productive, Successful You: End Procrastination by Making Anxiety Work for You Rather Than Against You".

Dr. James Claiborn, Ph.D., ABPP, is a Diplomate in Counseling Psychology from the American Board of Professional Psychology, and a Diplomate and Founding Fellow of the Academy of Cognitive Therapy. He is in independent practice in South Portland, ME specializing in treating OCD and related disorders and also licensed as a psychologist in New York, New Hampshire, Maine, and Deleware. Dr. Claiborn is a Founding Member of The Society for Sleep Behavioral Medicine, as well as a member of the Scientific and Clinical Advisory Board of the International OCD Foundation (IOCDF). Dr. Claiborn has presented on OCD, CBT and other topics internationally. He is the author of two self-help books; one on habit change and the other on body dysmorphic disorder.

Dr. Fred Penzel, Ph.D., is a licensed psychologist who has specialized in the treatment of OCD, OC spectrum disorders (including BDD, Trichotillomania, and Excoriation Disorder), and anxiety disorders since 1982. He is the founder and executive director of Western Suffolk Psychological Services in Huntington, NY, a private treatment group specializing in OCD and O-C related problems and is a founding member of both the International OCD Foundation (IOCDF) and Trichotillomania Learning Center (TLC) Science Advisory Boards. He is also a member of the advisory board of the United Kingdom's Anxiety UK organization. Dr. Penzel is the author of two books: *"Obsessive-Compulsive Disorders: A Complete Guide To Getting Well And Staying Well,"* and *"The Hair Pulling Problem: A Complete Guide to Trichotillomania"*. Dr. Penzel is also a frequent contributor to IOCDF's newsletter and *In Touch*, the newsletter of TLC.

Ethan S. Smith is a successful writer, director, producer, and author. Diagnosed with OCD at age 14, Ethan's functioning was significantly impaired due to his mental illness and lack of proper treatment available. After graduating high school, Ethan went on to attend the prestigious Meadows School Of The Arts at SMU on an acting scholarship only to drop out three months later, the OCD was too debilitating. Ethan continued to struggle throughout his twenties but still managed a very successful acting career. He appeared in over 150 commercials, guest-starred on television shows like "Dexter" and "CSI: Miami", and films like "Big Trouble", "Recount", and "I Love You, Man". At the age of 31, Ethan became unable to function and was bed ridden, riddled with OCD and anxiety. After 17 years, Ethan finally received life changing treatment in 2010. Fueled by a desire to prevent the suffering he endured for 32 years,

Ethan has approached his advocacy with honesty and brutal vulnerability. In just seven short years, Ethan gave the keynote speech at the 2014 annual OCD conference in Los Angeles, became a National Spokesperson for the International OCD Foundation, and currently serves as their National Ambassador. He has written countless articles and given numerous interviews for many major publications and media outlets. Ethan just completed writing a major feature film which he is now producing.

About the Author

Ryan Bernstein is a seventeen-year-old high school student with OCD. He is the founder and facilitator of Hand in Hand, a weekly OCD support group where he helps teens who struggle with anxiety learn new coping skills. As a youth advocate for OCD, Ryan seeks to educate and empower people through his writing and public-speaking. He has been featured in national blogs and newsletters such as the International OCD Foundation, and the Peace of Mind Foundation. Ryan encourages taking charge of OCD by helping others.